LEADERSHIP GENIUS

LEADERSHIP GENIUS

40 insights from the science of leading

RUS SLATER

ABOUT THE AUTHOR

Rus Slater has always been interested in leadership: military, commercial, religious, not-for-profit, sporting or even what is now known as 'thought leadership'. After a military career (as a leader), he moved into civilian employment and specializes in the areas of personal and leadership development.

He now defines, designs and delivers leadership and management training to organizations as diverse as Royal Colleges and motor dealerships, the civil service and global service companies. He also provides leadership to teams of the highly paid and the unpaid in commerce and the third sector.

Rus has also written seven other business books, sold globally in several languages as well as the original English.

Rus leads a delightful life in rural Hampshire.

'An easy, back-pocket read for any serious business leader or manager. The 'big takeaways' listed at the end of each chapter are a really useful resource. Slater presents the evidence that when it comes to leadership personal example, communication and knowing your people are key.'

Lt. Gen. John Lorimer

'*Leadership Genius* is a well-researched read bringing together both traditional and more contemporary studies into an engaging, often humorous, and most certainly accessible observation of the art of leadership. Recommended for both those who are new to leadership and the more seasoned practitioners.'

Mark Heywood, Senior Manager,
Performance Management Policy,
Lloyds Banking Group

First published in Great Britain in 2015 by Hodder & Stoughton. An Hachette UK company.

First published in US in 2015 by Quercus US

British Library Cataloguing in Publication Data: a catalogue record for this title is available from the British Library.

Library of Congress Catalog Card Number: on file.

Paperback ISBN 978 1 47360 927 3

eBook ISBN 978 1 47360 928 0

1

The publisher has used its best endeavours to ensure that any website addresses referred to in this book are correct and active at the time of going to press. However, the publisher and the author have no responsibility for the websites and can make no guarantee that a site will remain live or that the content will remain relevant, decent or appropriate.

The publisher has made every effort to mark as such all words which it believes to be trademarks. The publisher should also like to make it clear that the presence of a word in the book, whether marked or unmarked, in no way affects its legal status as a trademark.

Every reasonable effort has been made by the publisher to trace the copyright holders of material in this book. Any errors or omissions should be notified in writing to the publisher, who will endeavour to rectify the situation for any reprints and future editions.

Typeset by Cenveo® Publisher Services.

Printed and bound in Great Britain by CPI Group (UK) Ltd., Croydon CR0 4YY.

John Murray Learning policy is to use papers that are natural, renewable and recyclable products and made from wood grown in sustainable forests. The logging and manufacturing processes are expected to conform to the environmental regulations of the country of origin.

Hodder & Stoughton Ltd
Carmelite House
50 Victoria Embankment
London EC4Y 0DZ
www.hodder.co.uk

CONTENTS

INTRODUCTION

Is 'leadership' an art or a science?

Are 'leaders' born to lead, or can 'leadership' be taught?

These are two perennial questions that have long been debated, probably since the first time a human sharpened a stick and walked out of the cave saying 'Follow me!'

The concept of leadership as a birthright has been the topic of much debate for socio-political reasons, and now, in the 21st century, it is generally accepted that leadership represents a series of skills that can be learned, and exercised, much like any other intellectual and practical set of behaviours.

Again, there is much debate about what that set of skills and behaviours actually constitutes. This is then generally overlaid by the political considerations of the day; it is rare that Pol Pot, SS generals or Genghis Khan are referenced as 'good' leaders.

Every good bookshop (actual and virtual) has shelves of books on leadership, most of them written (or at least ghost-written) by military, political and business leaders, aiming to tell their leadership story.

While many of these books are a cracking good read, and many will teach useful leadership lessons, they tend to be very fixed in the time and the place in which the leader himself or herself lived. They tend to be anecdotal and driven as much by individual personality as by any objective analysis. Many of them define leadership in philosophical terms; their leadership was an art, rather than a science.

Most years there is a steady flow of more 'scientific' papers that are published by academics, consultancies and businesses. These range from weighty tomes with thousands of pages of statistical analysis to simple and straightforward survey results. Some are the product of a large team, months (or even years) of dedicated effort and large research grants. Others seem little more than a vehicle to issue a press release. Many of these papers are published and then never heard of again. Some become the basis for other work and some become misquoted, distorted and hence dangerous.

This book aims to provide something of a one-stop-shop by way of a reference to a selection of 40 of these more 'scientific' studies. I put the word 'scientific' in inverted commas for one reason. Science is, ironically, not an exact science when it comes to human behaviour; some scientific studies, while carried out with objective rigour, can be misleading, simply because of the nature of the study group. A study of behaviours and reactions may seem to be very comprehensive but then, when you dig beneath the surface, you discover that the observations and conclusions are based on a sample group of 15 people. Out of a population of 7 billion so this hardly counts as a statistically significant number.

Alternatively, the study may have had a larger study group but one that was homogenous; many popular, recognized and respected studies were carried out by American universities in the 1960s. The study groups were often other students and the student population of the time was almost exclusively educated, white, male and from a similar, middle and upper income socio-economic background.

The UK's Science Council exists to advance science in the UK but it realized quite early on that there was no adequate definition of what 'science' constituted.

It came up with the following definition:

'Science is the pursuit and application of knowledge and understanding of the natural and social world following a systematic methodology based on evidence.'

This is great, now we have a base definition of what constitutes science so we can separate the scientific conclusions from the homespun philosophy.

Why does this matter? TV news and documentary programmes are always telling us that 'scientists have discovered X', or that 'the evidence clearly states Y...' and generally we take their content as read, why? Chapter 1 looks at a piece of work that is already a couple of thousand years old. The theory it expounds explains neatly why 'science' is a powerful force in the leadership debate as well as being a lynchpin of many other issues that affect leaders and their followers.

Back to the Science Council. What it did next is quite interesting; the Science Council website quotes its definition and then provides a commendation of that definition by no other personage than Anthony Clifford ('A. C.') Grayling. Why does Grayling's opinion count? He is an MA, a DPhil (Oxon) and a Fellow of not one, but two, Royal Societies. Clearly he is a serious intellect.

But he is not a scientist.

He is a philosopher.

That piece of work in Chapter 1 also has some explanation of this. While we know that sometimes we can't argue with the actual evidence, we are generally also prepared to be influenced by people we can respect.

In recognition of the breadth of knowledge that a leader needs in the modern world I have not confined this book to studies that formally and solely concern themselves with 'leadership' in its purest sense. Leaders need to know about leadership, but they also need to know about human psychology, communication, motivation, marketing, how people learn and how customers behave and react. Consequently, this book is wide ranging in its base material.

It is also worth remembering that much science ends up being proven to be wrong; phrenology was once considered to be a respectable science but is now almost universally seen as a pseudo-science. Neuro-linguistic programming is hailed by some to be an irrefutable science while others decry it as mumbo-jumbo of the most dangerous sort. So much so in fact that, on many online forums, that single sentence would be enough to trigger a landslide of response and counter response that would go on until one party or another became so angered (and therefore unscientific) that their comments would be removed by the moderator.

Some of the studies included have been discredited or exposed as bunk; these I include simply because they are now so well known that they are seen as 'received wisdom'.

Finally it has to be said that many studies are carried out with less intention to find the answer than to simply act as a vehicle for the students to practise carrying out a scientific study. This means that many studies do no more than replicate previous studies. In consequence, this book may refer to one particular study; this is not to denigrate the others, simply to avoid the book reading like many scientific studies; with every single sentence referencing another academic's work in order to prove that the student has left no thesis unread and no textbook un-thumbed.

1 SPREADSHEETS ALONE DO NOT A JUDGEMENT MAKE

People make decisions based on factors other than pure logic... humans are no Vulcans!

Think about your private life for a moment.

Have you ever wanted something that you could *just* afford? This is something that you *wanted*, but didn't necessarily need. It could have been a car or a new mobile phone, an item of clothing or a holiday.

Did you buy it?

If so; why?

We all make judgements, whether in our purchases or our decisions to do things. Our capacity to make these judgements is not influenced solely by logical argument and demonstrable evidence.

And this is just as relevant in the workplace as in our home lives.

Aristotle, who lived from 384 to 322 BCE, was both a philosopher and a scientist. Born in Macedonia, the son of the personal physician to King Amyntas, he was probably at least in part brought up within a palace.

At 18, he moved to Athens and attended Plato's Academy where he remained until the ripe old age (for a student) of 37. He studied and mastered many subjects – including physics, biology, zoology, metaphysics, logic, ethics, aesthetics, poetry, theatre, music, rhetoric, linguistics, politics and government, and wrote on pretty much all of them.

So well known did he become as a scholar and sage that, in 356 BCE, King Philip of Macedon invited him to become personal tutor to his son Alexander, a job he continued to do for some 33 years. Not that Alexander was a slow developer but he was clearly a believer in 'lifelong learning'... even being known as Alexander the Great didn't dim the younger man's respect for his tutor.

Alexander gave Aristotle many opportunities both in regard to the areas of study and also the basic resources to store, collate and distribute knowledge. He established a library in the Lyceum, which aided in the production of many of his hundreds of books.

Aristotle immersed himself in empirical studies, hence is often viewed as humanity's first 'real' scientist. His works contain the earliest-known formal study of logic, which, in the late 19th century became the foundation of modern formal logic. He believed all people's concepts and all of their knowledge was ultimately based on perception.

Aristotle's work influenced Jewish, Christian and Islamic theological thought during the Middle Ages and he was revered by medieval Muslim thinkers as 'The First Teacher'. His work and thoughts on ethics have gained renewed interest with the modern (dare one say post-Christian) Western world and are still the object of active academic study today.

Aristotle's interest in politics and rhetoric led him to analyse the different ways that a proposal influenced people to make judgements and decisions.

He summarized his findings in what is usually referred to as his 'Model of Proof'.

This is pertinent for influencers both speaking to groups and interpersonal communication. In his day, of course, there was no electronic communication (mass media or individual), but the model stands the test of time and is still as valid in the 21st century as it was some 2,800 years ago.

It goes like this:

There are three elements that influence people:

Logos, the Greek for 'word', from which we get the word 'logic'

This refers to the *clarity* of the message's claim *and* the effectiveness of its supporting *evidence*.

The audience or other party should be able to both follow a *clear progression* of concepts *and* see reasonable and appropriate *facts* to support the message.

Ethos, the Greek for 'character', from which we get the word 'ethic'

This refers to the credibility of the speaker or writer or the credibility of the source from whence they may be quoting their evidence and facts.

If the audience is *personally* familiar with the speaker or writer, then that person's reputation with the *audience* will be critical. Is he or she an expert in the field? Does she have relevant experience?

If the speaker or writer is unknown to the audience, what evidence is there to suggest that the person is a knowledgeable expert? Remember A. C. Grayling? He has MA, DPhil, FRSA, and FRSL after his name; these post-nominal letters establish his credentials. Similarly, an august publication or institution can add ethos weight to a message: 'Source: *Harvard Business Review*', for example.

In the modern world ethos can also be added via the medium chosen to carry a message. 'As seen on TV' is a prime example, or the fact that the CEO makes a presentation personally is seen to add credibility over having an underling pass on the message.

Pathos, the ancient Greek 'suffering' or 'experience'

This is an appeal that draws upon the audience's emotions, sympathies, interests, and/or imagination. An appeal to pathos encourages the audience to identify with the message through their emotions; appealing to someone's better nature, tugging their heartstrings, emotional blackmail, sending them on a guilt trip, appealing to their self-interest are all examples of pathos arguments.

Think back to the opening paragraph of this chapter; did you buy something you wanted but didn't need? Logic said you didn't need it, but something else said you wanted to own it. It could have been that you just wanted to feel great by possessing it or it may have been that you know someone else who had one and so you felt if it was good enough for them it would be good enough for you. This is what people do; they are influenced by a combination of rational and emotional factors and they are swayed as much by the messenger as they are by the message.

OK, so there is the study. The question now is: 'What can you do to use that data to make yourself a better leader?'

People will only follow you if you influence them, so Aristotle's 'Model of Proof' is highly pertinent to your success as a leader.

Next time you want to influence someone, whether that person is a member of your team, a peer, a customer or even your boss, make sure you consider the logos, ethos and pathos of your argument.

1. Have you set out the factual evidence in a clear, concise and logical manner?
2. Have you established your personal credentials as an expert in this field (or, if you have no credentials in this field, have you made it clear that you aren't an expert? Owning up before you start is better than apparently being caught out later)?
3. If you are producing a slideshow presentation, have you considered not just the content but also the colour schemes (do they have adequate gravitas?), fonts and graphics?

4. Have you kept it brief enough to avoid 'Death by PowerPoint®'?
5. Have you practised it and rehearsed it so that you *maintain* your credibility?
6. Have you referenced all your logos arguments to credible ethos sources (remembering that, in some instances, the end users are the potentially most credible source; if you are recommending a corporate purchase on behalf of shop-floor workers, then the opinion of shop-floor workers is a very potent ethos argument). Have you taken into account the fact that 'credible' means credible to the audience not just to you; a reference to an American institution may go down well in some countries/with some audiences, but actually put people off in other places?
7. Have you considered all the pathos arguments that might influence each different member or group of your audience; what is in it for them? How will they *feel* about your proposal? Try to put yourself in their shoes to see what will make them feel good about your proposal; shop-floor workers are actually seldom that revved up about increasing shareholder dividend (unless of course they are shareholders) while customers are not really turned on by the idea of making managers' lives easier.

So what are the big takeaways here?

- **Next time you give someone an instruction or objective,** and they appear to be immediately prepared to accept it, ask how they *feel* about it (rather than what they *think* about it).
- **At the next meeting you attend as an attendee rather than as the chair, listen to the arguments put forward for different courses of action.** Assess each in the light of logos, ethos and pathos. If you see a colleague floundering because their argument is not 'three-dimensional', offer to share this chapter with them afterwards.
- **Remember the 'three Greeks': logos, ethos and pathos...** they really do help you to win people over.

Source

http://www.european-rhetoric.com/rhetoric-101/ethos-pathos-logos-modes-persuasion-aristotle

See also

Chapter 3 – It ain't what you say, it's the way that you say it

Chapter 20 – It sounds scientific and objective, but is it science?

Chapter 37 – 'Science, schmience'… take it with a pinch of salt

Chapter 39 – Trust in your virtual team

Further reading

courses.durhamtech.edu/perkins/aris.html

2 DO *YOU* REALLY KNOW WHAT MOTIVATES YOUR PEOPLE?

It is a sad fact that for a long time managers and leaders make erroneous assumptions about what motivates their staff or followers

Kenneth A. Kovach was a professor of management at George Mason University in Fairfax, Virginia in the US. As a professor of management he was, of course, motivated to study motivation and he carried out one such study in 1986.

It was carried out as a form of 'longitudinal study', not in that he surveyed the same group of people as previous studies but in that he asked the same questions in pretty much the same way as a study held 5 years beforehand and another, some 40 years before.

All three studies presented a set of ten factors that affect a person's motivation at work and asked the respondents to rank them in order of importance.

The factors were (in no particular order)

1. Good wages
2. Job security
3. Full appreciation of work done
4. Sympathetic help with personal problems
5. Interesting work
6. Promotion and growth in the organization
7. Personal loyalty to employees
8. A feeling of being involved in things
9. Tactful discipline
10. Good working conditions

Kovach found that the overall ranking given the factors in 1986 was significantly different from the rankings given in 1946.

Ranking	1946	Ranking	1986
1	Full appreciation of work done	1	Interesting work
2	Feeling of being in on things	2	Full appreciation of work done
3	Sympathetic help with personal problems	3	Feeling of being in on things
4	Job security	4	Job security
5	Good wages	5	Good wages
6	Interesting work	6	Promotion and growth in the organization
7	Promotion and growth in the organization	7	Good working conditions
8	Personal loyalty to employees	8	Personal loyalty to employees
9	Good working conditions	9	Tactful discipline
10	Tactful discipline	10	Sympathetic help with personal problems

OK, no great surprises there. 1946 was just after World War II, which followed the Great Depression, whereas 1986 followed a couple of decades of economic growth in the US. You'd expect people's motivators to change in line with the environment they work and live in.

One of the more interesting and valuable facets of all three studies was that alongside the questionnaire completed by employees was a similar questionnaire handed to their managers. This second questionnaire asked, not 'What motivates you?' but 'What motivates the people who work for you?' The results of this questionnaire remained completely unchanged from 1946, through 1981 to 1986. Great!

Consistency!

That is what we want, isn't it?

Sadly the managers' questionnaires may have been consistent across the managers and the decades, but they were completely at odds with the opinions of the people they purported to be about! The 1986 results looked like this:

Managers' perceptions of what motivates their people	People's self-declared motivators
1. Good wages	1. Interesting work
2. Job security	2. Full appreciation of work done
3. Promotion and growth in the organization	3. Feeling of being in on things
4. Good working conditions	4. Job security
5. Interesting work	5. Good wages
6. Personal loyalty to employees	6. Promotion and growth in the organization
7. Tactful discipline	7. Good working conditions
8. Full appreciation of work done	8. Personal loyalty to employees
9. Sympathetic help with personal problems	9. Tactful discipline
10. Feeling of being in on things	10. Sympathetic help with personal problems

Kovach was surprised that, though employees seemed to have changed considerably over the intervening years, managers' perceptions of employees hadn't. Bearing in mind that managers are employees too, and that the managers of 1986 were most unlikely to be the same managers as in 1946, this suggested that there was something that happened to people as they became managers that affected their perceptions.

Kovach postulated that managers may subconsciously upgrade the motivators that are outside their personal control when assessing what motivates people. This reduces their personal burden for motivation of their people, placing it more squarely with *their* bosses; wages, job security and working conditions are often company-wide schemes that individual managers have little influence over.

Another researcher has suggested that the management population simply 'projects' their own motivations upon the people who work for them. Since managers are generally promoted to being managers because they are presumably 'driven' and competent, they are more likely to be motivated by tangible measures. What more tangible measure is there than the size of your pay cheque?

The saddest fact in this is that, in spite of more than 40 years of research, most managers continue simply to copy their older and more established bosses' perceptions.

OK, so there is the data. The question now is: 'What can you do to use that data to make yourself a better leader?' Here are some suggestions:

1. When Kovach did his study in 1986 he also collected some personal data on the respondents. He found out that women often had a slightly different profile of motivators to men. (Generally, women put 'appreciation' above 'interesting work' at the top of the list.) He found out that employees (of either gender) had different profiles depending on age and position on their life path ('money' and 'job security' was often ranked higher among the younger respondents and 'loyalty' higher among the older ones). So rather than take the raw data as Gospel, make up your own mini-survey using the same 10 factors and use it with the people you lead. Find out what actually motivates your people rather than making a wild guess or an informed presumption. Then remember that as a person's life changes, their motivators may well change as well. Whenever someone in your team:

   • marries (or enters a stable relationship);
   • starts a family (or gets a ready-made one with a new partner);
   • becomes a carer for an older relative;

- has a partner whose circumstances change or;
- loses a partner (to death or divorce).
- This is the time to reassess what motivates them. Subtly and diplomatically, don't do what one boss did and, on being told that a staff member's spouse had just walked out, smiled and said: 'Oh, great, well you'll be looking for a lot more overtime now you have no home comforts to rush off to!'

2. Find out what each of your people finds 'interesting'. Just because you find spreadsheets wildly exciting, it doesn't mean that other people do too. Again, ask people what particular jobs they find interesting and try, where possible, to provide them with interesting work. If there are boring jobs to be done, try to rotate them, and take a leaf out of the British Royal Household's book below.

3. Ask yourself: 'When was the last time I showed my appreciation to a member of my team for something they have done?' If it wasn't in the past working day, ask yourself whether that is motivating your people (because appreciation of work done is #2 on the generic list!). You don't have to award someone a medal to show appreciation, you just have to say a few words: 'thank you', 'nice job', 'high five'. Some people will like to have it done in public and others will die of embarrassment if anyone else hears... but they should hear it! Show your appreciation if a member of your team does a good job for a customer and the customer is too rude to say thanks... it is motivating to know that someone noticed and had the decency to say something.

Remember that most of the important things that motivate your people are actually in YOUR gift. Don't be persuaded that only the HR department or the finance director can motivate people; people will work for YOU if you motivate them, in spite of the organization's lousy wages.

At the Summer Opening of Buckingham Palace, the temporary 'wardens' stand two in each of the many public rooms. They have been trained and educated in security and art history so they are fully briefed in the event of an incident or a question about any of the thousands of works under their eye. They are dressed in heavy wool three-piece uniforms, they must stand. They may not put hands in pockets; they are like the guardsmen outside but without the rifles and bayonets.

Most of the visitors rent an electronic talking guide, so the wardens may only get one or two questions per eight-hour shift. Potentially it is the most boring job in the world! Every 15 minutes each warden rotates to a different room or a different duty; they may be supervising the entry queue, or standing in a stateroom. They may be operating the 'Rapiscan' security system or searching bags. They may be leading a special tour or frisking visitors.

Their managers have gone out of their way to make a potentially boring job interesting.

So what are the big takeaways here?

- Next time you hear a fellow manager moaning about the lack of motivation in his or her team, share this chapter with them, pointing out that almost all the real motivators of human effort are within their grasp as a line manager.
- Sit down and take a look at your personal behaviours in the past week. Have you shown appreciation to every member of your team in that time? If not, get up, and go and find something to be grateful for!
- Remember in the future that a word of thanks, a gesture of personal appreciation and an explanation of the bigger picture, from you, is worth far more than an incentive scheme from the HR department.

Source

homepages.se.edu/cvonbergen/files/2012/12/What-Motivates-Employees_Workers-and-Supervisorys-Give-Different-Answers1.pdf

See also

Chapter 11 – To follow me they have to be able to see me, right?

Chapter 21 – Management and leadership... a hot topic! But for whom?

Chapter 23 – We're working nine to five – it's no way to make a living

Chapter 33 – Find out what your followers think about you, and talk to them about it!

Further reading

www.businessballs.com has a wealth of information about the topic of motivation

Morrell, Margaret & Capparell, Stephanie, *Shackleton's Way: Leadership Lessons from the Great Antarctic Explorer* (Viking Penguin, New York, 2001) is an excellent and inspiring read to see motivation in the face of unimaginable adversity

3 IT AIN'T WHAT YOU SAY, IT'S THE WAY THAT YOU SAY IT

You may be surprised to learn that this commonly known communication 'fact' is, in fact, fiction!

It is virtually received wisdom that:

- Only 7 per cent of communication is conveyed in the words we use;
- That 38 per cent of the meaning of our message is down to the 'tonal influences' – the tone, pace and volume with which we speak;
- And a whopping 55 per cent of communication is down to body language.

You will have probably heard commercial trainers, communication specialists, school teachers and voice coaches all quote these statistics.

They have been used in TV adverts for organizations as diverse as banks and perfume manufacturers. In fact they are probably the single most quoted statistics relating to communication and they are definitely in the Statistical Top Ten quoted numbers.

But...

Do you know their origin?

Were you aware that they are a very filtered and altered version of the original?

Are you aware that they are so altered as to be almost complete bunk!

The original and blameless source of this 'factoid' is Dr Albert Mehrabian, Professor Emeritus of Psychology, University of California, Los Angeles.

He came to psychology with a Bachelor of Science Degree and an MSc in engineering from the Massachusetts Institute of Technology. He received his PhD from Clark University and began his career of teaching and research at UCLA in 1964.

His background in engineering provided him with a distinctly empirical approach to his work. Knowing that it is only possible to test the validity of ideas by clear measurement, he has devoted much of his 50-plus years of research to the development of metrics and major theoretical models for measuring and describing complex psychological phenomena.

In 1981, Mehrabian published a book entitled *Silent Messages: Implicit Communication of Emotions and Attitudes*. This was based largely on experiments he had carried out to assess the comparative impact of different elements or factors on *the communication of attitudes and feelings*. In the experiments the subjects listened to, and watched, assistants saying particular words in particular tones of voice with particular facial expressions. The subjects then reported their impression of the underlying attitudes and feelings of the assistants.

Mehrabian's findings were as follows:

- **7 per cent of the message pertaining to feelings and attitudes is in the words that are spoken.**
- **38 per cent of the message pertaining to feelings and attitudes is conveyed in the tonal influences; the way that the words are said.**
- **55 per cent of the message pertaining to feelings and attitudes is in facial expression.**

These are in bold to make them stand out; they are the true ones rather than the oversimplified and misquoted conclusions.

Sadly, this is often simplified and distorted to read:

- 7 per cent of communication is conveyed in the words we use.
- 38 per cent of the meaning of our message is down to the 'tonal influences', the tone, pace and volume with which we speak.
- 55 per cent of communication is down to body language.

Why is it important that we are aware of the distortion?

Mehrabian was not looking into the 'meaning' of communication, but the underlying perceptions of *attitude and emotion*. By leaving out the qualification that attitude and emotion is the target, it is easy to make erroneous conclusions such as:

- Written communication can never be as effective as face-to-face communication.
- A telephone conversation cannot possibly convey the same meaning as effectively as a face-to-face conversation.
- If you want someone to understand you then you really need to be in the same room as them when you are talking to them

However reasonable those statements may sound; they are NOT reasonable conclusions from Mehrabian's work.

If the following words are said:

'Fire on the third floor, evacuate the building immediately.'

They clearly convey a universally understood meaning, and no differences of tone or facial expression are likely to change the way in which the meaning is understood. It is of course possible that the look on the face of the person saying them, and the tonal influences with which they are being said, may indicate that person's specific emotional reaction to the message, but the message is clear regardless.

Many other, more everyday business messages can be conveyed via words alone without any loss of *meaning*: straightforward factual messages, data, historic performance reports, descriptions of processes and straightforward instructions.

Mehrabian's experiments looked solely at face-to-face, verbal communication. None of the experiments used telephone communication (where, in theory, the tonal influences would have existed but with no non-verbal elements). However, it is not unreasonable to draw the conclusion that telephone calls do in fact potentially hide that latter aspect.

Neither did he look into written communication in any form, though his work is often cited as proof of the danger of misunderstandings arising in memos, letters, texts and emails.

Why is it important to be aware of the real outcomes of Mehrabian's work?

As a leader you want people to follow you. Their act of following you is a matter of *their* choice and it is NOT the same as you dragging them kicking and screaming behind you. You want them to do as you ask and as you would want. You want them to do it willingly, happily and with self-motivation and self-assessment so that they don't need to be permanently and consistently monitored.

This means that you are going to have to convince them that you really care about, trust and value them. You are going to have to convince them about your underlying attitudes and emotions.

You are also going to need to be convinced that they really are self-motivated and self-assessing. You are going to have to learn to see through the meaning of people's words and read their tonal influences and non-verbal behaviours to understand their attitudes and emotions.

Note that the term above is 'leader' rather than hierarchical figure of authority; when a US police officer points a 9mm automatic pistol at you and yells at you to lie face down on the floor and put your hands on your head, it is a fair bet then he or she isn't asking you to enter into a debate about the rights and wrongs of the US constitution, the merits of an armed police force or his or her attitude towards zero-tolerance law enforcement.

As a leader you are going to want people to follow particular courses of action; to be prepared to make significant changes in their working pattern; to put the needs of customers, shareholders and colleagues on the same footing as their own interests. You are going to have to persuade them to trust you, to believe in you and to take your word for things. This means you have to give them the impression (at least) that you care, that you are committed, that you believe in what you are saying and that you will keep your promises. All these things are emotions and attitudes.

OK, how much of this is relevant to you? Whether you are already the CEO of a large organization or a relatively junior manager you still regularly interact face to face with your own team. If you are in the former camp then your team interacts with immediate subordinates and so on down the line. If you are in the latter camp, you are interacting directly with the people at the 'coalface'. In either case you need to convince your direct reports of your bona fides.

If you have a 'chain of command' under you it is important to ensure that the links in that chain are all aware of the effect that their tonal influences and non-verbal behaviours have on your message that they are cascading through the organization.

The understanding of the importance of conveying your attitudes and emotions when speaking, and how to interpret the attitude of others when listening, will always be essential for effective face to face, verbal communication in management.

Here are three things that you can do to help you in relation to this:

1. Make a very conscious effort to have face-to-face discussions with as many people as you can to ensure that your attitudes of commitment, dedication, concern, respect and drive are clearly and accurately communicated.
2. Think about the tonal influences that will help you to make a connection with these people and improve the likelihood of their 'getting' your underlying attitude. Think about the non-verbal factors as well. Consider the PEOPLE mnemonic that you will find referenced in the **Further reading** section below.
3. Pay attention to the reactions other people have to you; listen to their words, be aware of their tonal influences and observe their non-verbal behaviours. This will give you the opportunity to assess your success as well as gauging their attitudes to you and your ideas.

So what are the big takeaways here?

- **Next time you hear someone misquoting this research, put them right... diplomatically!**
- **Before you send an email... stop!** Ask yourself if you might have your attitudes or opinions misconstrued through the lack of non-verbal elements.
- **Keep in mind the importance of making your tonal and non-verbal behaviours match your words...** if they don't people will see through the words or reach wrong conclusions about your underlying motives.

Source

Mehrabian, Albert, *Silent Messages: Implicit Communication of Emotions and Attitudes* (Wadsworth Publishing Company, Belmont, 1981)

See also

Chapter 12 – It takes all sorts to make a world

Chapter 16 – Getting engaged means committing and staying the course

Chapter 31 – Meetings (n); Events where people get together (eventually) and waste a lot more time than they need to

Chapter 36 – Stop paying attention to the PowerPoint® default settings!

Further reading

The PEOPLE mnemonic; available at www.coach-and-courses. com/page8.htm

4 I READ IT, BUT WHAT THE HECK DID IT MEAN?

There are many ways to write in English... sadly, many people choose to write in impenetrable English!

As management evolved throughout the past couple of centuries, managers wanted to 'professionalize' their field of endeavour. Management colleges and management qualifications started to appear. Management institutes were formed and managers started to style themselves like the other professions – doctors, lawyers and accountants.

Doctors use a lot of Latin. Yes, there is a reason for it; it crosses international and cultural boundaries and is clearly understood by an American doctor, a Russian doctor and an Arabic-speaking doctor. But it also confuses the rest of the mere mortals of the human race who do not have the benefits of a classical or medical education.

Lawyers, traditionally, notwithstanding previously established precedent, when communicating with similarly qualified individuals, and within legal boundaries, will usually eschew using diminutive taxonomy if there is a more long-winded and circumlocutory way of expressing their opinions which, of course are their personal opinions and are not necessarily to be accepted as the opinions of their publisher per se, who takes no responsibility for any damage, illness, injury or loss, regardless of magnitude that may be incurred as a result of listening to what they said.

In other words, professionals love to exclude people who aren't part of their clique.

Sadly, many managers follow this and write in a way that leaves the reader wondering what the heck they are going on about.

The 'readability' of documents is as important as the actual content.

Numerous studies in the 1940s showed that even a small increase in readability could greatly increase readership and circulation of newspapers.

In 1947, the publication *Wallaces' Farmer* used a split-run edition to study the effects of making its content easier to read. It found that simplifying the language increased readership by 43 per cent, a gain of 42,000 readers in a circulation of 275,000. This was on an article that was of lesser relevance to the readers. The study also found a 60 per cent increase in readership for an article that was more directly relevant to them.

Researcher Wilbur Schramm interviewed more than a thousand people about their reading habits. He found that an easier reading style helps to decide how much of a piece of writing is read. This was called 'reading persistence' or 'perseverance'. He also found that people will read less of long articles than of short ones. A document that is nine paragraphs long will lose three out of ten readers by the fifth paragraph. A shorter story will lose only two.

Rudolf Flesch, an Austrian-born American, was a 'readability expert', writing consultant and author who was a staunch advocate of plain English in the United States. A graduate of Columbia University, he earned a PhD in English and shortly afterwards published (in 1955) what became his most famous book, *Why Johnny Can't Read: and what you can do about it*. This is a critique of the then fashionable new practice of teaching reading by what was often called the 'look-say' method. In Flesch's opinion the flaw with this method was that it required the reader to have learned words by sight. When confronted with an unknown word, the reader was stymied. Flesch advocated a revival of the old-fashioned phonics method, the teaching of reading by sounding out words.

Flesch was a prolific author. He published many books on the subject of clear, effective communication and the relevant one to this chapter is *How to Test Readability*, which was published in 1951.

He devised, tested and proved the Flesch Reading Ease test. This is one of a pair of commonly used 'readability' metrics, the other being the Flesch-Kincaid Grade Level.

The Grade Level allocates an appropriate US school system academic grade level (eg school students aged x to y) to any piece of writing. The objective is to allow teachers, parents and librarians to make a judgement about the appropriateness of a title for their particular child or group. We will say no more about this test specifically.

The two tests were adopted by, initially, the US military for testing the readability of training manuals, i.e. the ability of a reader to actually understand what the manual was supposed to be teaching. Then they were adopted for all Department of Defense documents. Pennsylvania then made it a legal requirement that motor insurance policies be tested to be readable by anyone over the age of 15. The tests are now so widespread in the US that they are embedded as a default on Microsoft Word® (and many other proprietary word processors) spellchecking systems.

Sadly, many executives are unaware of this hidden gem!

The Flesch Reading Ease test uses a complex mathematical formula that crunches the number of words in a piece of writing with the number of sentences and also crunches the number of syllables with the number of words. It then does some magic with some constants and produces a nice, easy-to-see score, known as the Flesch Reading Ease Score or FRES.

The FRES is a simple number; the higher the number, the easier the piece is to read. It does exactly what it says on the tin. That boxed paragraph above scores minus 45... in other words it isn't easy to read and understand. That passage was deliberately written to be gobbledygook but I have just run the test on a passage written by a company director which aims to teach managers the performance management process of the company. It scored 26. Once he had re-written it in the light of the test score it scored 73... much easier to read and therefore more likely to be read, and subsequently more likely to be understood and more likely to be used.

The nice thing about the Flesch Reading Ease test is that the score is a simple number; the higher the number the easier the text is to read. You need no knowledge of the US school system to understand it. Of course 'scientists' don't all speak with one voice on any topic and readability is no exception. There are various other readability tests that are similarly well proven. SMOG is the 'Simple Measure of Gobbledygook'... this calculates the number of years in education required to read a piece of text, so again it is free from a link to the US education system. SMOG is the preferred measure of NIACE, the National Institute of Adult Continuing Education. It is also very popular with the Royal College of Physicians in the UK and the Health Department in the US.

This book 'plugs' the Flesch Reading Ease score simply because it is already at the fingertips of most executives.

> Sadly Flesch's last work was *Why Johnny Still Can't Read: A New Look at the Scandal of Our Schools*, which was published in 1981.

OK, that is the science, what can you do to put it to good use?

First, test your own work: to test a piece of writing on your PC (in Word®), simply follow the instructions below:

1. Save your work.
2. In the toolbar go to the Review tab
3. Select Spelling & Grammar
4. Change or ignore all the things that the spell checker identifies

5. After the last item you will get a dialogue box that contains your work's readability statistics:

- The first section is the 'Counts'; it counts the number of words, characters, paragraphs and sentences.
- The second is the 'Averages'; it calculates the average number of sentences per paragraph, words per sentence and characters per word.
- The third section is the 'Readability'; first, it simply tells you the number of passive sentences and then, by crunching the numbers via a complicated mathematical formula, it tells you the FRES. You want this number to be as high as possible. It also shows the Flesch-Kincaid Grade Level, which you should aim to get in the region of 9.

(If this doesn't happen then you probably have the Readability Statistics turned off... go to Review>Spelling & Grammar>Options... tick the check-box Show readability statistics, which needs to be enabled first in Word 2010...

1. Click the File tab, and then click Options.
2. Click Proofing.
3. Under When correcting spelling and grammar in Word, make sure the Check grammar with spelling check box is selected.
4. Select Show readability statistics.

Get into the habit of doing this regularly. If your scores are 'bad', download the NIACE free readability guide entitled 'How to produce clear written materials for a range of readers'. You can find the address at the end of this chapter in Further reading. The guide is only 12 pages long. Read it and use the advice in the guide to improve the readability of your work. Basically, think shorter sentences. Short words. More paragraphs.

So what are the big takeaways here?

- **When you get a document from a colleague and you have to read it twice to make sense of it, ask them what it scored on the readability test.** Share the way of getting a test score via their word-processing package or the online test mentioned below in Further reading. Ask other people to test their work. It is an eye-opener for many people!

- **Get into the habit today of testing your own work;** producing material that is difficult to read is NOT a demonstration of your own intellectual superiority... it is better to 'blind them with your brilliance, than to baffle them with balderdash'.
- **Remember; short paragraphs, short sentences, short words...** people have short attention spans!

Source

en.wikipedia.org/wiki/Readability

See also

Chapter 26 – Learning; it's a generational thing

Chapter 36 – Stop paying attention to the PowerPoint® default settings!

Chapter 40 – You can NOT be serious!

Further reading

office.microsoft.com/en-gb/word-help/test-your-document-s-readability-HP010148506.aspx#BM11 will help you to set up the test in Word® or Outlook®

https://readability-score.com allows you to carry out a test on a piece online

read-able.com allows you to test a website by simply putting in the web address

shop.niace.org.uk/readability.html offers a free readability guide in pdf format. Although it repeatedly refers to 'people with reading difficulties', it is a good primer for all business writing

5 'WORKERS' PLAY TIME' – IS IT REALLY WORTH IT?

Machiavelli said that a leader should instil fear in his followers. In this more enlightened age, perhaps making them happy works better

Ever since the human race moved (largely) from subsistence to employed economies there have been several questions that crop up repeatedly. Whether leaders are born or made is one, and another is whether people really are more productive when they are happy.

Read many organizations' 'vision and values' statements and you will find some reference to making their staff (or associates or employees or whatever they are calling them) 'happy'. There is a mass of anecdotal evidence that suggests that happy people are productive people, but there is little empirical evidence that this is true.

A study carried out over several years by the University of Warwick in the UK and the IZA (Institute for the Study of Labor) in Bonn has filled this gap.

'Happiness' was measured by a questionnaire which asked the subjects to provide a rating score of their happiness. This was repeated three times at strategic moments during the experiments. Clearly this is entirely subjective, but then so is happiness!

'Productivity' was measured by a paper-based arithmetic test. The subjects were asked to carry out simple additions of 5 two-digit numbers. They were allowed ten minutes to complete as many as they could, correctly. This was designed to replicate a white collar, office job rather than a manufacturing production role. The subjects were both male and female and were exclusively university students; so all had a level of education appropriate for office-type roles.

The subjects' productivity was assessed at the outset and then at the end.

The study ran in four separate experiments with a group sample of 713 people.

Experiments 1, 2 and 3 were carried out in controlled environments and subjects were paid piece-rates, in real money, for their correct answers; it was a real test of productivity for reward rather than a notional assessment of 'motivation'.

The individual experiments were repeated over six separate days to obtain 'longitudinal' data rather than being a one-off, and results were compared to check their validity. The different repetitions of the individual experiments were done at different times of the day to remove any effects of people's biorhythms.

The awareness of the *actual* financial reward for productivity was varied. The subjects were sometimes initially unaware of the actual detail of the financial reward; similar to many real-life jobs where connecting effort and success to financial outcome is blurred. In Experiment 2 the reward was made explicit to see what differences this would produce.

Corporate-sponsored 'happiness'

The 'happiness' was provided by a variety of different stimulants. These were deliberately selected to be things that an employer could provide or replicate at a relatively low investment. They ranged from video comedy clips to the provision of chocolates, fruit and soft drinks.

In all cases, control groups provided comparative data.

Happiness isn't just down to the boss though

Experiment 4 assessed the effect of real-life trauma on people's happiness and therefore their productivity.

The researchers didn't inflict any actual real-life trauma on anyone!

All subjects completed the aforementioned questionnaires which, among other things, asked them about their real-life situation and any 'Bad Life Events' (BLE) they may have been subjected to. These included:

- close family bereavement
- extended family bereavement
- close family life-threatening illness, and
- parental separation or divorce.

Those who had suffered/were suffering one or more BLEs which affected their happiness during the experiments could therefore be measured against those who were unaffected by these universally recognized events.

Is the received wisdom that happy people are more productive borne out by the science?

Experiment 1... comedy and laughter and implicit performance-related reward

The reported levels of pre-experiment happiness were virtually the same for both the subject group and the control group.

On average, people who were 'subjected' to the comedy clip were then 13 per cent more productive than the control group.

Gender seems to have had no impact: males and females showed little difference in the increase in productivity.

Some subjects (only 16 out of 276 or 5 per cent) reported that the comedy clip did not make them any happier BUT interestingly it had no effect on their productivity, they were as productive as the control group.

Experiment 2... comedy and laughter and explicit performance-related reward

In this experiment the subject group of 104 people scores 22 per cent higher productivity than the control group. The subject group males score very slightly higher than the females, but the difference in gender result was very small.

Experiment 3... chocolate, fruit and bottled spring-water. And explicit performance-related reward

In this experiment with 74 subjects it was found that there was a 15 per cent increase in productivity above the control group.

Experiment 4... subjects who had recently suffered a BLE or were in the midst of one

179 people took part in this experiment. They rated their happiness some 7.25 per cent less happy than people who are not affected by a BLE.

A very recent BLE had an effect, around 10 per cent less productivity if the BLE was in the past 12 months. This decreased over time and ceased to have any noticeable effect after three years.

The results above are simplified and summarized (the actual report is 43 pages in length). They mention productivity only as *successful* outputs; there were significant increases in people's 'effort' when happier; the number of 'attempts' also rises with 'happiness'.

The report's authors also accept that the short-term increase in happiness, and the corresponding increase in productivity, is not proven to be sustainable. They also accept that there has to be a cost/benefit analysis of the methods that might actually make people happier in the real business environment in relation to the percentage increase in effort and productivity. Inevitably, they suggest that further research is needed in this area (thus keeping them in jobs in academia for a few years more!).

As usual, there is the data; what can you do about it?

1. First, spread the news! Tell your boss and your fellow managers about this... it is the logos and ethos argument to the pathos (see Chapter 1) we have all been feeling for years!
2. Find out what will make your people happier; perhaps you could share the findings with them and ask them what they'd suggest as alternatives to comedy clips and chocolates. Once you know what this particular group would find

happy-inducing you can look to see if you can provide it
economically.

3. Find out what things have the opposite effect; what are the
   real-life, everyday 'buzz kills' that make them less happy and
   therefore less productive? Once you know what sucks the
   fun out of life for your people you can try to make sure you
   avoid it.
4. Do this on a regular basis; not just in a fit of enthusiasm that
   then tails off and goes down in history as yet-another-flavour-
   of-the-month initiative. What makes people happy changes
   so keep on top of the situation. Variety is the spice of life.
   Consider appointing someone (and rotating the responsibility)
   to be the 'smile monitor'.
5. Expect people's effort and productivity to be affected by real-
   life BLEs, but note that a 10 per cent drop in productivity isn't
   the same as a 90 per cent drop!

At one stage of its meteoric growth, the company now
known as HCL Axon actually had a board director
whose sole job was to make sure that its staff enjoyed
their jobs.

The staff members were highly valued knowledge workers
in a very competitive industry where headhunting and
poaching were very common. The Director of Fun was
responsible for making sure that staff were kept happy even
though most of them worked away from home and from
the company's own offices on client sites.

So what are the big takeaways here?

- **Tell your management colleagues that it is official:** work is not
  a 'four-letter word', happy people can be busy people, and,
  yes, it is a manager's job to make his or her people happy.
- **Go out into your team's workplace today and count the**
  'smiles'... actually delay that. It is probably better to look for
  frowns, scowls and glum faces. If you find them, try to find out
  why. Take an interest in people's levels of happiness.

- **Remember that you may not be the 'Director of Fun',** but ensuring you make people's happiness a weekly objective will pay dividends in the short, medium and long terms.

Source

www2.warwick.ac.uk/fac/soc/economics/staff/eproto/
workingpapers/happinessproductivity.pdf

See also

Chapter 7 – 'An employee's workspace is his castle… or should be!'

Chapter 9 – Rule No. 1: Never volunteer for anything. NOT!

Chapter 13 – To be (here) or not to be (here), that is the question

Chapter 17 – Spartan or 'house and garden'?

Chapter 22 – Look after the victims but look after the survivors first

Chapter 40 – You can NOT be serious!

6 AS A LEADER, IT IS A MATTER OF PRIORITIES

As if senior managers hadn't got enough on their plates, they have a major responsibility to make themselves redundant

So, you are a leader.

You are expected to provide a vision of the organization's future.

You are expected to craft a mission statement for the people to achieve.

You are expected to inspire your employees, your investors and your customers.

You are expected to create an environment where your people can excel.

You are expected to be the primary ambassador for the organization.

You are expected to have solutions to problems

You are expected to do all this *and...*

Train the very people who are just waiting for the first opportunity to take over your job?

Seriously?

Isn't that completely counterintuitive?

Well, yes, according to Eli Cohen (former research director of the University of Michigan) and Noel Tichy (professor of management and organizations at the University of Michigan's Ross School of Business). But their research suggests that it is also a critically important role for a leader. Their research was published in 2007 in the book *The Leadership Engine*.

Their research took place over several years and took the form of in-depth interviews and study visits with the people concerned. Their subject organizations ranged from the virtually unique, such as the Special Operations Forces of the US military (the Green Berets, Navy SEALS and Army Rangers), commercial organizations in mature industries such as Royal Dutch Shell and General Electric, fast-moving technology organizations such as Compaq and Intel right through to not-for-profit foundations such as Focus: HOPE. The subjects were all US oriented but many with global workforces.

It is that global nature that makes the topic they address so important; in the world today your competitors are everywhere, technology moves fast and customers are more discerning... and fickle. Organizations have to move fast to simply stay in the same place, to prosper requires lightning speed. This means that organizations have to employ people who can take decisions at a far faster rate than ever before. One very telling comment in the book is attributed to Larry Bossidy, then CEO of AlliedSignal:

'Everyone in the world is doing the same things we are. For us to succeed we must get there faster, with better prepared people.'

What sets Tichy and Cohen's work apart is that their research doesn't identify *what* you should be teaching people about the *details* of leadership. It does, however, clearly identify several important points about leadership and its development in the organization:

1. Leadership is important at *all* levels of the organization, not just at the top.

2. It is the leaders of today who should be actively developing (personally and devotedly) the leaders of tomorrow.
3. Today's leaders must have a 'teachable point of view' if they are to develop the leaders of tomorrow.
4. The 'teachable point of view' becomes a 'story'.

1. Leadership in not the sole prerogative of people with rank

In the past the world moved more slowly. Customers were less demanding, technology was slower and change was the exception rather than the rule. Without social media there was no immediacy of feedback or criticism. In the present, decisions have to be made fast; by the time an issue has passed up through a traditional chain of command, a decision has been made and an executive order is passed back down through the chain of command it is too late. Either the customer will have gone elsewhere or the issue will have become a crisis.

This means that leaders (the ones with the rank) must change the culture to one where people below them have the ability and the confidence to make decisions. This often means making them without the benefit of perfect data. This requires the formal leaders to behave differently to the way they may have behaved in an autocratic world, as well as expecting the people below them to demonstrate traditional leadership abilities of analysis and decision-making.

2. Today's leaders make the leaders of tomorrow

Tichy and Cohen make the point that *time* is the most valuable tool with which leaders create new leaders. A great leader makes and takes the time to devote to developing the leaders of tomorrow.

- This may be actually blocking out many days in the year to stand up and teach the 'fast-track', 'high-potential' or 'talent' group; Roger Enrico of PepsiCo spent one hundred days of the business year running five-day programmes of up-and-coming leaders.
- It may involve attending debrief, feedback and coaching sessions directly with potential leaders, as Admiral Ray Smith did with the special forces men in training.

- It may mean being active on internal business forums to provide opportunities to share wisdom, as Jack Welch did at GE.
- It may mean writing books and teaching sessions on in-house leadership training programmes, such as Intel's Andy Grove did.
- It may mean facilitating the learner-leaders in Action Learning Sets, as Ameritech's senior management did; helping their potential leaders to contribute US$700 million in revenue generation or cost savings.

> Action learning is a process which involves a set of people using their knowledge and skills, assisted by skilled questioning and facilitation, to re-interpret old and familiar concepts and produce fresh ideas.

3. Today's leaders have to have a 'teachable point of view'

They can't just stand up and do it 'off the cuff'; there is a considerable degree of thought required. They have to analyse what, in their considered opinion, it takes for an organization to succeed in their particular area of work, and in the environment and marketplace that the organization is functioning in. They need to form a strong and comprehensive opinion about what it takes to lead the people that their organization employs. This may require them to spend time thinking about their own past actions and those of their colleagues. They may need to benchmark against other relevant organizations and compare differences. It will also require them to develop informed opinions about the future of the marketplace and the organization.

4. Creating a story from a 'teachable point of view'

Based on their considered opinion, the leader-teacher now creates a compelling story about where the organization has been and where it is going. It includes the elements of how it is going to get there as well. Then the leader-teachers tell that story and by doing so lead the leader-learners to help them to make it come true.

Tichy and Cohen make one very telling additional point, which is aimed at the HR or personnel community. Historically, in many organizations, the HR community has been the buyer of 'leadership' training. Leaders were busy leading and development was the responsibility of the HR function. This cannot continue as it effectively 'outsources' the parenting behaviours that create new leaders:

- Now HR has to identify the leader-learners.
- HR has to identify the leader-teachers.
- It has to help them to generate their 'teachable point of view'.
- It has to assist in creating opportunities for them to teach and tell their story.
- It has to be prepared to surrender its control of the learning and development of the leadership cadre of tomorrow.
- It has to convince busy senior leaders that they have the right and the responsibility to spend a lot of their time doing something that probably won't show on the bottom line for several years....

And all that takes a brave a HR director!

So what should you be doing to make use of this research?

A lot will depend on your current position in the hierarchy; if you are far enough up the organizational ladder to have a major impact, then start shaking the tree.

If you are in middle management you are more likely to be a leader-learner, so:

- Start actively seeking opportunities to learn from your bosses by planting the seeds of points 2 and 3 above in his or her mind.
- Actively encourage your bosses to spend some time outlining their story to you and your people.
- Encourage your bosses to set up and guide Action Learning Sets to help both improve operational issues and simultaneously expose people to the challenge of development.
- Make it part of your weekly to-do list to actively develop the leadership ability of the potential leader-learners in your team (it is probably actually already part of your job description, but is normally one that is reduced to asking HR what leadership or management courses are available and appropriate).

In reality you are probably also a bit of leader-teacher; you can learn from your superordinates and pass on their wisdom (and a bit of yours) to your team.

So what are the big takeaways here?

- Ask your boss to give you a brief summary of the five most important traits, in his or her opinion, of a successful leader in your organization. Don't expect an immediate answer; you want something considered, not 'off the cuff'.
- When you get this from the boss discuss it with him or her. How well do you reflect those five traits and what can you do to improve them? Think about your people; who is the current 'best match' in your team, and what should you be doing to develop that person and the others?
- Remember that developing the leaders of tomorrow is too important to be outsourced lock, stock and barrel to the HR department or an external consultancy.

Source

Tichy, Noel & Cohen, Eli, *The Leadership Engine: How Winning Companies Build Leaders at Every Level* (Pritchett, Dallas, 2007)

See also

Chapter 12 – It takes all sorts to make a world

Chapter 16 – Getting engaged means committing and staying the course

Chapter 26 – Learning; it's a generational thing

Chapter 29 – Is getting engaged really worth the effort?

Chapter 30 – Managing the millennials... some new challenges

7 'AN EMPLOYEE'S WORKSPACE IS HIS CASTLE... OR SHOULD BE!'

Allowing people to take responsibility for their own workspace may make your life easier and them more productive

Lots of organizations employ a 'clear-desk' policy.

Some forbid the decoration of workspaces with personal 'clutter'.

'Hot-desking' doesn't really allow for anything personal at all.

The spectre of 'Health & Safety' ensures that unregulated personal possessions can be banned.

Workplaces don't need 'art' and flowers; people are there to work, not to relax.

Logic dictates that the fewer distractions from your work there are, the more productive you should be.

Ah, but human beings are influenced by things beyond 'logos' arguments; remember Chapter 1? People are also influenced by ethos and pathos arguments. If they perceive that a credible organization somewhere else provides attractive pictures and nice carpets, they may feel that they are hard done by. This may result in a detachment from their employer and a reduction in job satisfaction.

So do people actually care about the environment in which they spend the majority of their working lives?

In 2010, Professor Alex Haslam and Craig Knight, of the University of Exeter, set out to establish a number of scientific truths relating to workplace decoration. They wanted to ascertain what effect a person's level of control over their own workspace had on their feelings of wellbeing and their identification with their employer.

The first study

Subjects for their first study represented four, fairly typical, private sector organizations: a transport company, an office services firm, an architectural practice and a firm of designers.

The people were based in 13 UK organizations and 3 in the USA. They represented a spread of hierarchies: 16 per cent were non-managers, 37 per cent lower management/team leaders, 34 per cent middle managers, and 13 per cent described themselves as senior managers. There were 116 women and 172 men. (Percentages have been rounded to the nearest whole number.)

They completed a comprehensive survey that assessed:

- How much *autonomy* they had over the day-to-day environment, such as whether they could control the heating in their workspace
- How much 'management' *involved* them in decisions relating to their environment, for instance, were they consulted over space use or not?
- How *comfortable* they felt in their workspace
- How much they *identified* with their employer and their managers
- How much job satisfaction and *enjoyment* they felt
- Their *wellbeing*, measured by such things as lighting-inducing headaches.

The results of this survey confirmed four important relationships between elements measured:

1. **The more managerial control there was, the less comfortable the employees felt.** So what? Well, this suggests that no matter how much management time, 'expert' advice and financial investment the organization devotes to workplace design, it is wasted... if the people who work in the workplace aren't involved and allowed some input.
2. **The more comfortable people feel at work, the more they identify with their organization and managers.** So what? If you want people to feel that they are part of your team and you are part of theirs, then their comfort is important. People who identify with their employer, and YOU, use their initiative and act with integrity.
3. **The more people identify with their employer, the higher their levels of job satisfaction and enjoyment.** So what? Job satisfaction and enjoyment are things that keep people motivated and productive. This makes your job of managing them easier!
4. **The more people identify with their employer, coupled with higher levels of job satisfaction and enjoyment, matched with higher levels of wellbeing.** So what? People who report higher levels of wellbeing generally have higher attendance and less claim for time off sick. So in the short term (your day-to-day and week-to-week management) and the long term (employee turnover and organizational 'sick day' costs) there is benefit to gain.

The overall message is one that is slightly counterintuitive:

'Stop taking on the burden of being "responsible for managing" people's work environment; allow and encourage them to do it for themselves.'

Knight and Haslam recognized that 4 organizations and 288 people may not actually represent a significant sample. So they carried out another study.

The second study

In this study there were 1,643 subjects with a split of 66 per cent male and 34 per cent female. Within this group, 55 per cent described themselves as non-managers and 5 per cent as senior managers with the remainder falling into the junior/middle management level. This was felt to be a more significant overall size of sample as well as being more reflective of the real working population. 90 per cent of the respondents were based in the UK with the remaining 10 per cent spread around the rest of the globe.

The results of this survey replicated, almost exactly, the first study.

To put it graphically:

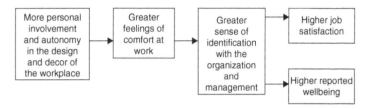

The report's authors are clear that, though the connections seem clear, there are obviously other, unassessed factors in play; a greater sense of comfort alone will not guarantee a greater sense of identification with the organization and more job satisfaction. Autonomy over the work environment does not in and of itself improve employee wellbeing. But it is certain that autonomy and comfort are contributory factors to people's job satisfaction and their health and welfare in office environments.

So much for the science, what can you do about it to improve your lot as a manager?

First, take a fresh pair of eyes to the workplaces that your people inhabit.

1. It is quite probable that lots of your people sit in open-plan offices. If so, what is there to delineate one person's domain from that of their next-door neighbour? If there is no way

to tell who sits where, this suggests that there is not a lot of autonomy in regard to people's workspaces.

2. Take a look at the differences between work time and the time when the office is closed (in the evenings or at the weekend). Is there any noticeable difference? If the place is stark, bare and functional even when there are employees present this might suggest that the place could do with some personal touches.

3. Look around the workspace. What colours are obvious? Look at the floor, walls and any room dividers. Are they a drab shade of neutral and boring? The following is received wisdom among designers; **orange** – stimulates creativity; **yellow** – intensifies the intellect and heightens motivation; **red** – energizes; **blue** – is calming, fights physical and mental tension; **green** – fights irritability and has a healing effect on the body.

4. Take a deep breath. Does the air seem clean and healthy or stale? The Environmental Protection Agency in the US estimates that 6 out of 10 buildings are 'sick' with regard to the indoor air quality and that this is America's top environmental health problem. A recent study by the US Department of Agriculture found that ionizing a room led to 52 per cent less dust and 95 per cent less bacteria in the air. Small negative-ion air purifiers are available for a fairly modest price.

5. Look up. What is the light like in the working environment? Studies suggest that natural light increases both human productivity and reduces tiredness. If your workplaces have fluorescent tubes, investigate replacing them with full-spectrum tubes. These emit a balanced spectrum of light that is the closest you can get to natural sunlight. This eases eye fatigue, helps fight Seasonal Affective Disorder and reduces cortisol stress hormone levels.

6. Look underneath your people. What are they sitting on? Does it suit them? Are seats set at the right height for comfort?

But...

Don't take on the task of doing all this alone, get the team involved. Ask the staff what they'd like to change about their workplace environment to make it more comfortable and more. Invite them to contribute to making these changes. Give them some control over the workplace.

So what are the big takeaways here?

- Ask people what would be their 'perfect working environment'...
- Then help them to help you to create it...
- But avoid treading on their input, even when there are divergent views.

Source

www.sciencedaily.com/releases/2010/09/100907104035.htm

See also

Chapter 13 – To be (here) or not to be (here), that is the question

Chapter 16 – Getting engaged means committing and staying the course

Chapter 17 – Spartan or 'house and garden'?

8 'WHAT'S "LUCK" GOT TO DO WITH IT?'

Luck isn't as random or as fleeting as you might think...
or as the unlucky might claim

Some people are just born lucky; they get all the breaks, they get the great job, they get the promotions, they happen to be in the right place at the right time to shine on the fantastic projects.

Other people are rather like Jonah. They seem to always miss out on the opportunities, everything they do turns to dust, they seem doomed to a life of disappointment and mediocrity.

Humbug!

Scientifically proven to be humbug!

Professor Richard Wiseman is professor of the public understanding of psychology at the UK's University of Hertfordshire. He has carried out extensive research into the concept of 'luck' and its effect on people's personal and working lives. To this end he went out into the real world and asked people who considered themselves either exceptionally lucky or exceptionally unlucky to take part in his research. More than 400 people took part, ranging in age from an 18-year-old student to an 84-year-old retired accountant. People from all walks of life were represented: entrepreneurs, blue-collar workers, educators, administrators, homemakers, medical professionals and sales professionals.

Wiseman subjected them to a battery of tests, interviews and searches over a period of several years. He got them to complete diaries, undertake personality and intelligence tests, and to take part in laboratory experiments.

For example, Wiseman gave his subjects a newspaper and asked them to look through it and tell him how many pictures were in it. The 'unlucky' people took just two minutes on average to come up with the right answer. The 'lucky' people did it in just a few seconds! How? The 'lucky' people noticed that on the second page was a half-page announcement written in two-inch high letters that read: 'Stop counting – there are 43 photographs in this newspaper.' The potential 'lucky break' was staring everyone in the face, but the 'unlucky' people missed it, whereas the 'lucky' people saw it. When a subject saw it and reported to the experimenter, they were told 'well done, but you might as well keep looking through the paper'. They then almost all noticed that Wiseman also posted another, same-sized message, half-way through the paper. This one read: 'Stop counting, tell the experimenter you have seen this and win £150.' Most of the 'lucky' people won this cash bonus. In spite of having looked at this page, hardly any of the 'unlucky' people spotted either of the opportunities; they were only searching for photographs.

Wiseman noticed that the 'unlucky' people had far higher scores for anxiety and tension in their personality tests. Anxiety is known to disrupt a person's ability to notice the unexpected. 'Unlucky' people, being tense, tend to be so intent on looking for something specific, that they simply miss other opportunities because they aren't the specific thing being sought. For example 'unlucky' people miss the opportunities for a better job because they are so busy looking for a particular job advert.

This covers the element of 'noticing' chance opportunities, but what about 'creating' them?

Wiseman discovered that 'unlucky' people often seemed to stay 'stuck in a rut'; they often seemed to stay within the same circle of work acquaintances, they had a circle of personal acquaintances that remained constant. They tended to frequent the same workplace year after year, and go to the same social places repeatedly. They were creatures of habit... and this reduced their likelihood of being in the right place at the right time in order to 'notice' a chance opportunity. 'Lucky' people on the other hand, either unconsciously or consciously, varied their routines, did different things, and thus were exposed to a wider variety of opportunities.

His conclusions were that the concept of 'luck' as a happenstance, over which a person has no influence, is complete humbug. More usefully, he also identified four basic principles that so-called 'lucky' people employ, often unconsciously, that generate positive outcomes. The failure of the so-called 'unlucky' people to be aware of (and use) these principles is what often leads them to the negative outcomes that they ascribe to 'just my typical bad luck'. Here are the first two principles.

Maximize chance opportunities

First, lucky people are skilled at creating, noticing and acting upon chance opportunities. They do this in various ways, which include building and maintaining a strong network, adopting a relaxed attitude to life, and being open to new experiences. Wiseman reported one example of a 'lucky' person who when going to any function deliberately decides to meet with different types of people; he will choose a colour and then, if the colour was, say, red, deliberately seeks out and speaks with everyone wearing a red item of clothing. It may sound bizarre, but it breaks a habit and opens up new opportunities.

Listen to your lucky hunches

Second, lucky people make effective decisions by listening to their intuition and gut feelings. They also take steps to actively boost their intuitive abilities – for example, by meditating and clearing their mind of other thoughts.

Wiseman also found that there was a distinct difference between 'lucky' people and 'unlucky' people in the way they viewed opportunities and incidents. People who described themselves as 'lucky' had a general tendency to look on the bright side of events actual and historical:

'I was so lucky: I was involved in a car crash and my arm was broken badly, but I lived, no one else died, and I also met some really nice people.'

Conversely, 'unlucky' people tended to view the same event as solely negative:

'It was just my luck! The car was written off, I received a badly broken arm and was in hospital for ages, and then back and forth to hospital without a car!'

Wiseman found that this perception on the part of both groups coloured their view of the future; the 'lucky' people, got up, brushed themselves off and went forward expecting some degree of success, whereas the 'unlucky' people tended to restrict their future activity in the anticipation of failure... or bad luck.

Wiseman also draws some inferences with regard to events that are not necessarily associated with good or bad luck. He talks of someone winning a bronze medal and looking at it on the basis of the success of getting into the medal zone, whereas the silver medal winner is thinking that only a tiny extra bit of effort would have put them on the top of the podium.

This led Wiseman to principles 3 and 4.

Expect good fortune

Thirdly, lucky people are certain that the future will be bright. Over time, that expectation becomes a self-fulfilling prophecy because it helps lucky people persist in the face of failure and positively shapes their interactions with other people.

Turn bad luck to good

Fourthly, lucky people employ various psychological techniques to cope with, and even thrive upon, the ill fortune that comes their way. For example, they spontaneously imagine how things could have been worse, they don't dwell on the ill fortune, and they take control of the situation.

So there are Professor Wiseman's findings (Wasn't he lucky to have been born with the name 'wise man'; almost a guarantee that he'd end up as a professor!)

He created a luck school, where he teaches people certain techniques to improve their 'luck'. One simple and easily replicated thing that he does is have people keep a 'luck diary'. At the end of each day, 'students' spend a couple of moments writing down all the positive and 'lucky' things that happened that day. They are banned from writing down the negative and/or 'unlucky' stuff. After doing that for a month, it's difficult for them not to be thinking about the good things that are happening. Almost all 'students' report significant improvements in their lives, both professional and personal.

It is almost a dead cert that you will have a few 'unlucky' people in your team. They may not consciously declare themselves to be unlucky but you can spot them from some of the types of things that unlucky people do and say as reported above.

So what are the big takeaways here?

- Next time you hear a team member or a colleague looking solely at the negative outcomes or possibilities of an experience, tell them about this research.
- Get a copy of Wiseman's book (the details are listed below under Source), read it yourself, pass it round the team and get them all to read it. Hold a weekly meeting to replicate the 'luck diary' mentioned above.
- Remember that 'luck' doesn't exist... people wittingly or unwittingly make their own good and bad fortune.

Source

Wiseman, Dr Richard, *The Luck Factor* (Arrow, London, 2004)

See also

Chapter 10 – The five-step ladder to increased success

Chapter 12 – It takes all sorts to make a world

Further reading

www.fastcompany.com/46732/how-make-your-own-luck

www.richardwiseman.com/research/psychologyluck.html

uhra.herts.ac.uk/bitstream/handle/2299/2289/902384.
pdf?sequence=1

9 RULE NO. I: NEVER VOLUNTEER FOR ANYTHING. *NOT*!

One volunteer is worth ten pressed men

No sexism intended; just historical realism. The term 'impressment' originated within the Royal Navy in the days when the service required men to crew its ships. The unfortunates were 'press-ganged' by sailors against their will – basically kidnapped into a lifetime of servitude at sea.

Virtually everyone will have heard someone say that the first rule in life is to never volunteer for anything. But is there any value in allowing, or even encouraging your people to volunteer to do things? Things that might distract them from achieving the goals and objectives you set them (or agree in partnership with them)?

Myriad studies over the first decade of the 21st century have suggested that, far from distracting people, it is a 'good' thing to allow and encourage them to volunteer in the community.

In the UK, Business In The Community (BITC) has two declared aims with regard to the matter of employee volunteering:

1. To develop and embed the vision for every business to achieve excellence in their community programmes.
2. To significantly increase the positive impact of business in the communities of greatest need.

Which is all very well, but... 'excellence' in the first aim isn't a guarantee of value to the business. And the beneficiary of the positive impact in the second aim isn't the business, it is the 'communities of greatest need'... so does a business get anything out of this relationship? If times are good, and a business is flush with money, then yes, it is nice to give something back, but is there a bottom line value to the business that will sustain this philanthropy when times are tougher?

BITC has produced a summary entitled 'Employee Volunteering Business Case'. It sets out the bottom-line benefits to organizations that they can gain from encouraging their employees to undertake voluntary work. The summary draws on a wide range of studies and research predominantly from the UK but with some international data included.

The BITC report sets out these benefits in five distinct areas that would be relevant to virtually any business leader:

1. **Consumer image** – Community Service Volunteers carried out a survey in 2013 and found that 88 per cent of the British public is more likely to buy from an organization that is seen to support and engage in activities to improve society.
2. **Recruitment and career progression** – Deloitte's report 'Talent Edge 2020' found that a prospective employer's commitment to sustainability was 'important' or 'very important' to 92 per cent of all potential recruits and 63 per cent of 'millennials' or Generation Y (people aged between about 16 and 31). YouGov found that 1 in 3 recruiting managers (in the private sector; and 61 per cent of public sector managers) rated volunteering as an asset when seeking to fill a vacancy.
3. **Employee morale and performance** – YouGov's 2010 document, 'Volunteering is the Business' found that 71 per cent of employees who did voluntary work in their spare time (with support/encouragement from their employer) declared that this was key to improving their personal wellbeing. 85 per cent of them reporting that their perception of their employer was improved by the support they received.

4. **Learning and development** – YouGov reports that managers and employees consider volunteering activities as beneficial to improving people's problem-solving skills, their self-confidence, their communication and listening abilities, and team-working. All this provided at little or no cost to the employer.

5. **Local image** – Volunteering is usually centred around the local community, raising the profile of a business in its own locale. This has benefits with regard to attracting local recruits, local suppliers and local customers.

So that is what the research tells us; what can you do about it?

There are two ways to extract value from this collection of studies:

Personally, as an individual

Volunteering is valued by many recruiting managers in both the public and private sectors, so getting experience as a volunteer will stand you in good stead in the future. Consider offering your current work skills to a charitable organization. Many professions and trades have a clearing house for this activity; some are run by the members' institutes and some as individual not-for-profit organizations. There are also several generic clearing houses such as volunteeringmatters.org.uk and www.do-it.org.uk. Examples might be mentoring, book keeping or providing training.

Alternatively, you can select a charitable organization that is geographically attractive or operates in a relevant field. Here you have choices as well. You can learn new skills such as first aid, acting as a guide for visitors or operating specialist equipment. You could simply use your donation of manual labour to keep you fit and healthy. Most regions also have volunteer branches of their emergency services; you can become a paramedic, police officer, firefighter or soldier; these opportunities tend to provide world-class formal training programmes and recognition.

Managerially, as a boss

Employees tend to feel more engaged with their employer when the employer supports them in their desire to 'give something back'. Charitable volunteering also provides free training and personal development opportunities for your people, making them more valuable to you as an added benefit. So encourage people to volunteer, either individually or as a group.

Chris managed a team of people for an organization. They worked hard, each concentrating on their individual desk-bound role, dealing with their customers over the phone or by email. There was little opportunity for bonding as a team.

Chris instigated a two-day off-site to get people working together in a different environment to break down barriers and engender some team ethos. Instead of going to a posh hotel and spending a lot of money climbing trees or banging on bongos, Chris arranged for them to redecorate the accommodation of a local charitable boarding school for severely epileptic children. The charity paid for all the materials and Chris's team provided the workforce. The cost to the employer was solely the team's salary.

The project was a success in terms of team bonding, the charity benefited to the tune of several thousand pounds of savings, team members saw several of their colleagues shine in a different light, demonstrating strength of character previously unseen and a number of the team members continued in a volunteering role with the school afterwards.

So what are the big takeaways here?

- Spread the word that volunteering isn't just for 'bleeding hearts' and 'ladies who lunch'; it brings value to those who volunteer, those they help and society as a whole.
- Give people time and encouragement to volunteer in whatever capacity they wish to or are able to.

- **Remember that:**

  The quality of mercy is not strained;
  It droppeth as the gentle rain from heaven
  Upon the place beneath. It is twice blest;
  It blesseth him that gives and him that takes:

Source

www.bitc.org.uk/issues/community/employee-volunteering

Business in the Community: 137 Shepherdess Walk, London N1 7RQ 020 7566 8650 information@bitc.org.uk

See also

Chapter 5 – 'Workers' play time' – is it really worth it?

Chapter 16 – Getting engaged means committing and staying the course

Chapter 29 – Is getting engaged really worth the effort?

Further reading and resources

https://vinspired.com/media/W1siZiIsIjIwMTQvMDMvMTEvMT
cvMjcvMDQvMjEyLzA2XzA3XzQ0Xzc4N19Wb2x1bnRlZXJJp
bmdfaXNfdGhlX0J1c2luZXNzX0ZJTkFMLnBkZiJdXQ

www.csv.org.uk/?display=volunteering

www.deloitte.com/assets/Dcom-UnitedStates/Local%20
Assets/Documents/IMOs/Talent/us_talent_talentedge2020
employee_042811.pdf

10 THE FIVE-STEP LADDER TO INCREASED SUCCESS

A goal shared is a goal made a lot more likely to be achieved

When I first left the army in 1987 I was employed in a sales role. I attended a training course and one of the trainers was an extremely successful salesperson and sales manager, who also happened to be female, young, pretty and blonde. She was earning around £84,000 *a month*.

In a session on the setting and achieving of goals, she informed us that a 1953 study at Harvard University had found that only 3 per cent of a specific group of people wrote down their life goals. Twenty years later that 3 per cent were earning, on average, 10 times more than the people who didn't express goals or didn't write them down. When she started out she had set her heart on owning a Porsche 911 sports car. She had made a label that looked like this:

9:11

She stuck it over her current car's digital dashboard clock so it always reminded her of her goal.

One of the delegates on the course, a 50-something-year-old man, had taken a rather oppositional view of this particular trainer (he was not positively influenced by her 'ethos' – see Chapter 1), and questioned her about the 'provenance' of this study, claiming that he knew for a fact it was actually conducted at Yale University.

In fact, they were both wrong; the whole matter was a very plausible-sounding urban myth of unknown origin, as was proven by Dr Gail Matthews (Dominican University of California) and Steven Kraus (Harvard University) in the later 1990s. The discovery did, however, lead Matthews to undertake a similar study herself.

Matthews made the study more robust than the legendary condition of write or don't write and she shortened the target period from 20 years to 4 weeks.

She recruited 149 people – 37 men and 112 women, aged between 23 and 72, and based in the US, the UK, Belgium, India, Australia and Japan. They were all in paid employment in public and private sectors, and represented a fairly wide range of levels of authority and responsibility.

They were divided randomly into five groups and each group was set a different condition, as outlined below.

Group No.	Condition	
1	Simply **think** about what they wanted to achieve over the four-week target period and **consider** its difficulty, importance, whether they had the skills and resources to achieve it, their commitment and motivation, prior attempts and prior success.	
2	Everything asked of Group 1, plus...	...make a **written record** of their deliberations
3	Everything asked of Groups 1 & 2, plus...	...formulate **action commitments** to move them towards the achievement
4	Everything asked of Groups 1, 2 & 3, plus...	...**send** the written record of goals and action commitments to a 'supportive friend'
5	Everything asked of Groups 1, 2, 3 & 4, plus...	...**send** weekly progress reports* to that **supportive friend** (* this group was sent weekly reminders to send the progress reports)

Individuals in all groups had the freedom to select their own real goals to achieve and they ranged from pure work-related goals, to career goals, and ambitions related to wellbeing. For example:

- completing a project (including completing a chapter of a book, updating a website, selling a house, writing a strategic plan, winning a contract, recruiting staff and preventing a hostile takeover)
- increasing income
- increasing productivity
- getting organized
- enhancing performance
- improving work/life balance
- reducing work anxiety and learning new skills.

At the end of the four-week period all the individuals were asked to score themselves on a scale of 1 to 10, to reflect the level to which they had succeeded in achieving the goals they had set themselves.

The outcomes are shown below as the mean score for each group.

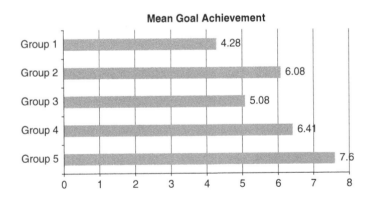

To put the outcomes into words:

- Your likelihood of achieving a goal is enhanced by 26 per cent if you write down your goal.
- Your likelihood of achieving a goal is enhanced by up to 50 per cent if you engage in some form of action planning,

sharing and regular reporting. (Comparing Group 1 with a combination of Groups 2–5).

- Creating a series of action commitments in order to incrementally move towards the goals increases the likelihood of success by 18 per cent.
- Taking some accountability for success by sharing your goals with another person increases the likelihood of success by 49 per cent.
- Showing commitment to the accountability, by regularly reporting progress to that other person, increases the likelihood of success by 77 per cent.

Matthews terms the three elements of the experiment as:

- Written goals (written down and therefore more concrete than purely ethereal)
- Commitment to goals (thinking through a plan of action)
- Accountability (sharing the goal and progress towards it with another party).

There is the research; what can you do about it?

As a leader in the 21st century you undoubtedly already write down your goals and you almost certainly expect your people to write down theirs, even if only as an email communication. You also expect to get and to make regular reports of progress.

However, Dr Matthews' study didn't use the 'boss' as the person who subjects committed to and reported to but a 'supportive friend'... what is the difference?

A boss...	A supportive friend...
...has a vested interest and obligation to his/her boss to ensure goals are met.	...has no personal obligation to make sure that someone achieves but takes an altruistic interest.
...has the power of censure if either reports aren't produced, or if progress is deemed inadequate	...wants to see progress for the sake of the subject, no one else.
...is the boss in the eyes of the employee	...is a friend

So it is unlikely that you can realistically presume that the study equates directly to your relationship with your staff. Neither, if you are a senior manager, can you presume that your direct reports can take the role of 'supportive friend' with their staff.

'Supportive friends' are more likely to be co-workers in the same department and at an equal level in the hierarchy; former colleagues who have moved in, within or away from your organization; former colleagues from previous employers; or social friends and family.

Encourage your people to socialize informally among themselves. Allow people to take breaks and have 'water-cooler' conversations with co-workers. (Though perhaps unhealthy in other ways, the 'tobacco network' of smokers who network with people from other departments as they all huddle out in the rain to feed their habit, is often a great source of 'supportive friends'.)

Encourage a buddy-system to grow within the organization and beyond.

Employ external business coaches, or encourage cross-functional coaching.

Encourage the human resources and learning and development business partners to act as 'supportive friends'.

Assist your people in joining professional associations and institutes that have local chapter meetings where they can meet and form supportive relationships.

Think beyond your staff's day-to-day and quarterly goals; consider their life goals and their career goals. Encourage extra-curricular activity and corporate social responsibility.

Think beyond the organizational/operational goals that your boss sets and that you set yourself. Think about your life goals and your career goals. Achieving personal life goals makes people happier and more fulfilled, it usually also broadens horizons and makes for more rounded personalities. Having and achieving career goals makes people more successful and happier; not everyone wants to be the CEO, and that is good, but what do people want? Do they know what they want? People taking a greater degree of active interest and control of their careers may lead to them leaving you and seeking pastures new, but that is not necessarily a bad thing, especially if they remember that you were the person who helped them achieve their goals rather than yours!

So what are the big takeaways here?

- **Ask people to show you their written goals;** not just for this financial year but for their life, or at least the foreseeable future.
- **Change the screensaver on your computer or smartphone to a text message with your current goal on it;** this way you'll not only have written it but you'll have a constant reminder of it and other people will see it as well.
- **Remember that just writing down a goal increases the likelihood of achieving it by more than 25 per cent...** if someone came and offered to sell you the secret of improving performance by that much you'd be a fool not to listen.

Source

www.dominican.edu/academics/ahss/undergraduate-programs
-1/psych/faculty/fulltime/gailmatthews/researchsummary2.pdf

See also

Chapter 1 – Spreadsheets alone do not a judgement make

Chapter 8 – 'What's "luck" got to do with it?'

Chapter 18 – Leadership and leaders; let's get complex

Chapter 39 – Trust in your virtual team

11 TO FOLLOW ME THEY HAVE TO BE ABLE TO SEE ME, RIGHT?

Your people really can be more productive when you aren't there to manage them!

You know that your people don't actually need to have you in eyeshot all the time. But here is the real question; we live in the 21st century, with the Internet and personal computers, video conferencing, webinars, mobile phones and broadband. So why do we still have the majority of our people traipsing into the office every day to work?

Famously, Yahoo! banned working from home in February 2013, having been exponents of the practice for several years. Marissa Mayer, the decision-maker behind the ban wasn't echoing the cynics' cry that working from home was actually a charter for 'shirking from home'. She was aiming to increase the informal channels of communication that exist in a co-located workplace; the water-cooler conversations and the almost casual chats that she believed led to great ideas.

At least one disgruntled (but anonymous) Yahoo! employee took a different view, working from home meant that 'I didn't have to put up with numbskull self-important programmers constantly yakking to each other LOUDLY from the next set of cubicles about non-work-related stuff, and I wasn't being distracted every 20 minutes by some bored soul coming over to my desk to go for coffee or foosball [sic]...'.

A joint study by Stanford and the Beijing University School of Management looked at the whole issue of productivity of people working from home (WFH for short). This study was completed in Q3 of 2011 having run for nine months as a pilot programme. The results of the experiment were quite striking, albeit that the sample group, though quite large, was very homogenous; the people were all call centre operatives in the travel and hospitality sector from one organization.

Here are some basic facts about the study, each with some comment thrown in about them:

1. 996 employees were offered the opportunity to work from home four days a week and come into the office to work for just the one day. 503 of the people offered the option declared a serious interest... so 50 per cent of people wanted to work from home when offered the option and 50 per cent didn't.
2. Of the 503 people who wanted to, some did not meet the eligibility criteria. Those that did were divided randomly to create a WFH sample and a control group (people who wanted to work from home but weren't allowed to). The WFH group was provided with identical IT systems and workflows as their control group cousins. Both groups continued to receive an element of their remuneration as performance-based pay... so this study really does compare apples to apples with regard to the work done and the equipment; the only variable was the location.
3. Over the nine-month period of the study, the performance of the WFH group was 13 per cent better than the performance in the office. This was made up of several factors: first, they were actually working for longer in each shift (often due to the greater convenience, if you will excuse the pun, of a shorter distance to the loo, the kettle and the snack facilities); their productivity rate during each shift also went up (due to greater peace and quiet and fewer distractions). So this study suggests that people working from home actually worked harder and smarter rather than 'shirking from home'.
4. The control group's performance remained constant, in comparison to their previous performance and in comparison to other groups in the company who had never been offered and lost the opportunity to work from home. So it didn't raise an expectation and then rock the boat to investigate the option.

5. The WFH group reported far higher scores in job satisfaction and improved attitude towards the employer, leading to a whopping 50 per cent drop in staff turnover in comparison to the control group. So if you want to keep your good people and you want to keep them productive and they want to work from home... the advice seems to be to let them!

6. Interestingly, the study also noticed that WFH employees had a lower promotion rate... it was not investigated further to see if this was due to the organization not wanting to give extra authority and responsibility to people who weren't in the office or whether WFH people felt sufficiently fulfilled not to apply for greater responsibility and pay.

7. The employer reported that over the nine-month study they had saved approximately US$1,500 per employee (that would work out at US$2,000 per year). So not only does productivity rise, but costs fall as well.

8. After the study the employer decided to continue and expand the WFH option to all employees, including allowing the original WFH group to re-opt. Two-thirds of the control group opted to stay working in the office (in other words, they changed their minds from ten months beforehand)... the primary reason given was concerns over the loneliness of working without daily visual contact with their colleagues. Half of the WFH group chose to return to the office environment... most of these were the poorer performers but there were also some higher performers who were lonely. So though most people initially yearn for the 'freedom' of working from home, it isn't for everyone... but trying it out or seeing it in your close colleagues tends to help people make a sustainable decision.

9. After the experiment was over, the people now working from home returned a 22 per cent higher performance... almost double the experiment's result, suggesting that the more 'selective' the decision-making, the higher the benefits.

The report's authors are at pains to point out the homogenous nature of the work group and their particular tasks do limit the direct applicability of this study to the world of work in general. However, they also point out, and are right to do so, that some of the more generic findings can be assumed to be entirely relevant to a great many modern, office-related roles.

OK, there is the research and its findings, what can you do about it?

1. Do some research into the 'overhead' costs of providing a desk chair, office phone, heating, lighting, parking space, etc. for each employee in your team. Many managers and leaders are amazed at how much it costs an organization just to put a metaphorical 'bum on a seat'.

2. Ask your team to keep a record of the amount of time they lose due to unwelcome distractions. Make sure you let them know why you are doing this, otherwise they'll assume that you are just micromanaging them. Convert that time to a cost to the business.

3. Ask your team who would want to work from home, and for how much of the time. Tell them that you are considering the possibility of being more flexible about people's actual presence in work. Ask them to consider whether they have a suitable space to use, whether they have adequate broadband facilities (if applicable).

4. Investigate the specific IT needs with regard to security and data protection... almost anything is possible, though some very secure systems may be expensive.

5. Ask yourself whether you are prepared to trust the people in your team to work from home. The reality (from the study) seems to be that people are actually trustworthy, but that isn't necessarily the same as you actually having the trust in them!

6. Think back over the good people you have lost in the past; any that left due to pressures of home life, children's needs, elderly parents or distance of commute. Consider if you'd been more able to allow them to work from home for a couple of days or even the whole week whether they would still be with you.

7. Trial the situation: benchmark the situation in the office, set a review period, and then re-analyse at the end of the review period. Perhaps allow everyone (or the appropriate people) to work from home one or two days a week at the outset.

8. Get your own management style in order. Start thinking about ROWE (see Chapter 32), where people are not driven by staff calls and they need objectives and results to target.

9. Look into how to get the best from a remote team; can the water-cooler conversations still happen when you are hundreds of miles apart? But are they less casual and are you the person who needs to make them happen?

So what are the big takeaways here?

- **Tell people about this study;** the source is quite readable (though it is 45 pages long and does get a bit statistics heavy) and you could start or fuel a revolution.
- **Lead by example.** NOT by going home yourself, but by creating an environment where people (including you) can work from home, at least some of the time.
- **Remember that just because you can't see them working they probably are,** and just because they can't see you leading, you can still be doing so.

Source

https://web.stanford.edu/~nbloom/WFH.pdf

See also

Chapter 5 – 'Workers' play time' – is it really worth it?

Chapter 7 – 'An employee's workspace is his castle... or should be!'

Chapter 17 – Spartan or 'house and garden'?

Chapter 23 – We're working nine to five – it's no way to make a living

Chapter 39 – Trust in your virtual team

12 IT TAKES ALL SORTS TO MAKE A WORLD

One of the most dangerous ways to recruit is to recruit in your own image... too many 'people like us' is a recipe for disaster

You are a leader.

This implies (or even demands) that you have followers.

In some cases these followers may act simply as individuals, in isolation from each other with the only common denominator being their 'followership' of you.

Alternatively, you may have followers who act independently and, to add to their motivation, you encourage them to gently compete with each other; a sales 'team' might be a good example here. It is quite usual to find in this example that they all come from similar psychological moulds. They may have diversity of age, race, religion and sex but they have similar personalities and characters.

> Think of the TV programme *The Apprentice*... the candidates are all highly competitive, slightly sociopathic, egotistical and highly driven. It would make for rather dull TV if they weren't.

It is relatively easy to identify what will make for success and then stick to recruiting to that pattern.

The third option, and probably the most common, is that they, and you, bond together and you encourage them to cooperate with you and each other towards a single common objective. In this format, there is still competition as a motivator, but the competition is external, against other teams or other organizations.

The forerunner of the famous Henley Business School was called the Administrative Staff College. From the 1960s they ran a ten-week course for potential board directors where the delegates were formed into eight teams to run business simulations, each team operating as a commercial company and competing with each other. In 1969 they invited Dr Meredith Belbin to observe the teams in action. He built his own small team of professional researchers with differing specialist approaches and for the next nine years they observed, assessed, monitored and analysed pretty much every move the delegate teams made.

The outcomes of their research were first published in 1981 as *Management Teams – Why They Succeed or Fail*. Belbin continues to work in the field of management.

Belbin and his colleagues found that almost regardless of the intellect or the education of the individual team members, it was the balance of different team behaviours that was a greater contributor to whether a team became successful or not. They identified (eventually) nine different 'roles' that were critical for a team's future.

> The 'roles' are not necessarily each a different person, but each of the roles needs to be demonstrated regularly by someone in the team on a regular basis in order for the team to have the balance that predicates success.

A successful team in work (as opposed to sport) needs to have:

- Some creative, imaginative free thinking. Generation of ideas and problem-solving capacity. Belbin refers to this as **Plant** behaviour.
- Outgoing, enthusiastic, communicative. Exploration of opportunities and development of contacts. This is **Resource Investigator** behaviour.

- Maturity, confidence, identification of talent. Focus on goals. Effective delegation. This is **Coordinator** behaviour.
- Challenging assumptions, dynamic, thriving on pressure. The drive and courage to overcome obstacles. This is **Shaper** behaviour.
- Sober, strategic and discerning. Sees all options and judges accurately. This is **Monitor/Evaluator** behaviour.
- Cooperative, perceptive and diplomatic. Listening to others, averting conflict. Belbin labelled this **Teamworker** behaviour.
- Practicality. Turns ideas and thought into plans and actions. Organization of work that needs to be done. Reliability and efficiency. This is **Implementer** behaviour.
- Painstaking attention to detail, anxious enough to want to check and recheck things. Searches out errors. Polishes and perfects. This is **Completer/Finisher** behaviour.
- Dedicated relevant technical knowledge and determination to use it. This is **Specialist** behaviour.

Recognition of the need for these behaviours presents some interesting challenges to any manager or leader:

Completer/Finisher behaviour can be seen as nit-picking, or worse; looking for things to criticize. Shaper behaviour can be seen as negativity, stamping on ideas or on the person who came up with them. Teamworkers can be seen as fluffy peacemakers, more interested in everyone being nice to each other than in getting the job done. Coordinators can be seen as lazy because they delegate and Implementers can be seen as bossy.

Being a successful leader or manager requires you to accept these conflicts as healthy and to manage them, and the bruised egos, for the overall good of the team.

Belbin went on to develop assessment tools to help identify what primary behavioural preferences a person has for the relevant behaviours and these are exceptionally powerful for leaders and other team members.

A team in a bank's IT department was clearly having problems. Its current project was at serious risk of not coming in on time; one of their previous projects was a renowned disaster. There was constant friction between two different pairs of team members, which was just below the formal complaint-of-harassment level.

The team manager took the team for a facilitated off-site meeting to try to get them functioning. They all took a Team Role preference questionnaire. When they saw the results on the wall they realized that there wasn't a single person who had a preference for Completer Finisher behaviour. This was the primary cause of their past failure. Almost all of them had a strong preference for Plant behaviour and there was very little balancing Coordinator or Implementer behaviour.

Their new-found understanding helped them to sort out their differences (for the large part) and, without laying people off and recruiting new people they were able to start functioning a lot more effectively. They hit their next delivery date on time and to standard.

So, how can you get value out of this research? There are numerous different ways to exploit it:

1. Get a Belbin® Team Role report on yourself; this will give you the tools to do some self-analysis. Armed with the knowledge of your own preferences you can take a new look at your career choices. Given that many people are promoted to management positions based upon their technical knowledge, it may well be that you have little preference for the more 'leader-y' behaviours and knowing this will help you.
2. Still on the self-analysis front, you can now look at your attitude to other people; have you labelled others as bossy, when in fact they are simply Shapers? Have you disregarded someone's actions as overly critical when in fact they were doing the critical action of a Completer/Finisher?
3. If you have a team to lead at present, get a Team Role report for each team member. This will give you a good

understanding of the strengths and weakness of the team as a whole.

4. Share the explanation of the Team Roles with the team, since this allows them to self-assess and, as such, is a powerful way of improving teamwork.

5. Use Team Roles when you are looking to recruit; this will help make the team more complete and is infinitely better than recruiting PLUs (People Like Us – that is, recruiting in the image of the existing team)

6. When there is an incident, whether it is a problem in achieving a goal or a clash between team members, make a concerted effort to assess the behaviours of the members of the team to see if there is an obvious deficiency in any one or more of the Team Roles. Alternatively, is there too much of one particular behaviour? This is an excellent way to look at cause and effect. Obviously, once you find the real causes you can put a considered plan of action in place to prevent future problems.

Belbin's work is considered seminal in the field of teams and teamwork. His company, Belbin Associates, is still going strong in the consulting market and its product is used by many successful organizations.

So what are the big takeaways here?

- **Next time you hear someone moaning about a fellow team member** ask them what team role behaviour they think the person was exhibiting about which they are not happy.
- **Next time you feel that things are not going well in the team you are in** (the management team, or your own work team) look around and analyse the behaviours; is there an imbalance?
- **Remember that though 'birds of a feather may flock together', it takes all sorts to make a team function successfully.**

Source

Belbin, R. Meredith, *Management Teams – Why They Succeed or Fail* (Butterworth-Heinemann, Oxford, 3rd edition 2010)

See also

Chapter 6 – As a leader, it is a matter of priorities

Chapter 18 – Leadership and leaders; let's get complex

Chapter 20 – It sounds scientific and objective, but is it science?

Chapter 21 – Management and leadership... a hot topic! But for whom?

Chapter 39 – Trust in your virtual team

Further reading and resources

www.belbin.com/rte.asp?id=302 to buy Belbin Team Role reports online

For other resources, handouts, explanatory notes to share with the team www.belbin.com

13 TO BE (HERE) OR NOT TO BE (HERE), THAT IS THE QUESTION

Managers and leaders can have a major effect on people's sick records... you don't have to be a doctor to make people better

As a leader and manager you are responsible for the work productivity of your people in relation to the pay you give them.

Several other chapters of this book refer to the studies done into people's productivity when they are 'at work'. This chapter looks at a regular study undertaken to look at the situation when people aren't 'at work'. Why the inverted commas on 'at work'? This study looks at 'absenteeism'. That title was originally coined in the days when to be at work was solely and purely a matter of one's geographical location. The presumption was that if an employee wasn't at their place of work, then they weren't producing anything, but they were costing the organization their salary. Britain's Chartered Institute of Personnel and Development carries out a regular survey into the topic of absenteeism. They are looking not at physical location of the employee but the days when the employee is formally accepted to be non-productive. They are looking at staff sickness.

The 2013 report is based upon 618 respondent organizations from across the UK in June and July of that year. These organizations ranged in size from fewer than 50 staff to more than 5,000. In total the headcount represented was some 2.3 million employees. Respondents represented:

- the private sector in two guises: private sector services and private sector manufacturing and production
- the public sector
- the not-for-profit sector.

The survey sought data on absentee levels, cost of absenteeism, the causes of absenteeism and the rise in 'presenteeism'. (In this instance, presenteeism is defined as coming in to work when actually unfit to be there, rather than the alternative definition which is pretending to be present when in fact absent.)

Snapshots

Here is a brief selection of snapshots of information from the survey findings; some are included here because they are perhaps contrary to the received wisdom and some because they scientifically confirm matters that are otherwise blindingly obvious.

1. Levels of absence are higher in the public sector than in the private sector; the public sector loses an average of 8.7 days per employee per year, in comparison to 6.6 in the private sector as a whole.
2. There is a perfect correlation between size of organization and lost days per employee: the bigger the organization the more time people take off for sickness. (1–49 employees = 6.6 days per employee per year lost. >5,000 employees = 9.2)
3. Three-quarters of private sector days lost are due to short-term absences of fewer than seven days, in comparison to only half of the public sector.
4. Long-term absences (4 weeks or more) are three times more likely in the public sector than the private sector.
5. 60 per cent of public sector organizations have a formal target for the reduction of absenteeism.
6. The public sector reports a financial 'cost' of absenteeism per employee per year of £726, some 55 per cent higher than the private sector's £469... though it has to be said that it is comparing apples to oranges; the two sectors measure the cost in very different ways and so while the figures themselves are valuable, any comparison between sectors is actually quite meaningless.
7. Absence due to non-genuine ill-health (or, in the CIPD's own words, 'pulling a sickie') is nearly four times more likely for manual staff, and twice as likely for non-manual staff, in the private sector than the public sector. So the common belief that 'You wouldn't get away with that in industry' is wrong!

8. Stress is cited as the single most common factor across all employees for long-term sickness.
9. 'Volume of work' and 'management style' are cited as the two biggest causes of stress across the board.
10. 78 per cent of employers (who have taken any steps to manage presenteeism) have advised managers to send home staff who come in sick, and 56 per cent have made arrangements for staff to work remotely if the nature of their condition makes remote working appropriate.

Most usefully, the survey also asked what actions organizations were taking to counter and manage absenteeism. It then went a stage further, and asked respondents to rate the effectiveness of these actions. 'Manage' in this instance covers prevention/ avoidance as well as after-the-event actions. With regard to **short-term absence** these are the top five:

Most common actions	Most effective actions
1. Sickness absence information given to line managers	1. Return-to-work interviews
2. Return-to-work interviews	2. Trigger mechanisms to review attendance
3. Allowance of leave for family circumstances (carer/ emergency/dependent/ compassionate)	3. Line managers take prime responsibility for managing absence
4. Trigger mechanisms to review attendance	4. Disciplinary procedures for unacceptable absences
5. Disciplinary procedures for unacceptable absences	5. Sickness absence information given to line managers

The full options list in both cases was of 23 items including various 'cost implication' measures such as health benefits, employee assistance programmes and attendance bonuses. Interestingly, the five most effective actions are all measures that present no extra cost to the employer; they are about the line managers at the coal face doing their jobs a bit differently.

For long-term absences:

Most common actions	Most effective actions
1. Return to work interviews	1. Occupational health involvement
2. Changing work patterns or environment	2. Return-to-work interviews
3. Sickness absence information given to line managers	3. Changing work patterns or environment
4. Risk assessment to aid return to work after a long absence	4. Tailored support for line managers (e.g. online support care conference with HR)
5. Occupational health involvement	5. Restricting sick pay

This study is a 'longitudinal' one; the CIPD repeats it annually so the actual document contains a lot of comparative data relating this year to last year and identifying trends in the overall situation and in specific sectors.

So there is the research, what can you do to benefit from it?

Much will depend on your position within your organization. If you are a senior manager you can look at your organization's overall strategy for absence management. If you are a line manager you can be looking at the way you manage absence in your team and looking to see how you may *influence* the overall direction of the organization.

The first point to note is that absence management is not an HR issue; it is an issue for line management, be that at team, department, division or organizational level. In other words absenteeism is a leadership issue rather than an administrative issue.

Return-to-work interviews (RTWI) are very effective tools in managing both long-term and short-term absenteeism and they are completely within your remit.

Here are some best practice guidelines for planning and carrying out a return to work interview (remembering that they are the #1 'most-effective' tool in short-term absence management):

- Be familiar with the team member's attendance record (this also fulfils numbers 2, 3 & 5 of the 'most effective' measures for short-term absences).
- Carry out an RTWI after each absence; it doesn't have to be a big, formal occasion, a three-minute chat may well be adequate. Do it within a day of their return and do it in private, where you can both speak without interruption or being overheard.
- Welcome the team member back to work.
- Seek confirmation that they are fit to work (from the point of their own capacity and the likelihood of them affecting their colleagues).
- Investigate the cause of the absence.
- Remember that it is not necessarily your responsibility (or your right) to provide advice or a solution to the cause of the issue. It is your responsibility to minimize the effect it has on the performance of the individual and the team. So, without prying, and without trying to be a doctor or counsellor, try to offer solutions or refer the team member to support organizations (in house or open to the public).
- If the absence relates to a disability, pregnancy or a work-related accident, undertake a risk assessment and inform the HR function.
- Agree a review period and/or any actions required as appropriate.
- Make and keep notes confirming the RTWI; these may be needed in the future if the absences require more structured or more formal intervention and support.

If at any stage it becomes apparent that absence from work could be a matter of misconduct or performance capability rather than ill-health, seek advice from your HR function. (Which is moving you towards #4 in the 'most effective' tools for managing short-term absenteeism.)

So what are the big takeaways here?

- If one of your peer group mentions a team member of theirs who is absent ask them when they are planning on doing a return to work interview... if they aren't (or they aren't planning to follow best practice) tell them about this chapter and the report it refers to.
- If one of your staff takes time off then make sure you carry out an RTWI... it doesn't have to be a major event, but it shows that you have noticed that they were away and that you care.
- Remember that absence is not somebody else's responsibility; it is yours!

Source

www.cipd.co.uk/hr-resources/survey-reports/absence-management-2013.aspx

See also

Chapter 5 – 'Workers' play time' – is it really worth it?

Chapter 11 – To follow me they have to be able to see me, right?

Chapter 17 – Spartan or 'house and garden'?

Chapter 23 – We're working nine to five – it's no way to make a living

Chapter 32 – ROWE, ROWE, ROWE your boat!

Further reading

www.acas.org.uk/media/pdf/7/t/B04_1.pdf

14 LEADERSHIP IS NOT ABOUT BRAIN SURGERY YOU KNOW

It really can help a leader to have an understanding of the physiology of the human brain... even if you don't plan on cutting open your followers' skulls!

In November 2014 Britain's Chartered Institute of Personnel and Development published a report entitled 'Neuroscience in action, applying insight into L&D practice'. The report is aimed at learning and development professionals, but it is just as relevant to leaders in other disciplines for several reasons:

- They may be buyers of L&D services or products.
- They may be called on to design and deliver training of some description during the course of their working year.
- They have a day-to-day management/leadership responsibility for developing their team (especially their future leaders: see Chapter 6).
- Undoubtedly they themselves should be learning every day as well!

The report is based on a series of case studies and surveys within a specific group of eight organizations. They span public and private sector, domestic and international organizations. They are involved in manufacturing, utilities provision, professional services, leisure, financial services, healthcare and emergency services:

Organization	Description
Allens	A major international law firm
BT	A global telecoms company
Fitness First	A health club company with 377 clubs in 16 countries

(*Continued*)

Organization	Description
Imperial College Healthcare NHS Trust	6 hospitals and 1 college working together to form the UK's first academic health science centre and employing 10,000 people
SABMiller	A beverage and brewery organization employing 70,000 people in over 80 countries
Unum	A specialist financial protection insurance provider in the UK serving 1.6 million individuals and half of the FTSE 100 list of companies
Volvo	The automotive conglomerate employing 110,000 people in 19 countries
Welsh Ambulance Service NHS Trust	3,000 staff. 250,000 emergency calls per annum and 1.3 million non-emergency journeys

The report's authors wanted to identify what benefits an understanding of neuroscience was bringing to the layperson in work. Neuroscience is the study of the human brain and nervous system; the increasing sophistication and availability of such machines as fMRI (functional Magnetic Resonance Imaging) scanners allows scientists to 'see' brain activity and therefore to link cognitive and behavioural neuroscience to behaviours and learning within the workplace. The advantage of this approach is that it is cross cultural and free from language barriers; human brains in South Africa, Peru and Australia all work in the same way, as do the brains of lawyers and call-centre operatives.

The report cites numerous corporate results that the respondents put down largely to the influence of the use of neuroscience:

- Fitness First saw a staff turnover rate drop of more than 60 per cent
- The Welsh Ambulance Trust solved a problem that the organization had been grappling with for 20 years
- Fitness First has seen an improvement in its net promoter score of 15 per cent.

The report is clear (it appears in a highlighted text box on the second page of Chapter 1 which is regarding the value of neuroscience) that a fairly large amount of the neuroscience does little more than support what people already knew. As the authors put it: 'It helped to confirm their intuitions or validate their practical experience.' This is valuable in a number of ways:

1. It gives confidence by reinforcing beliefs and opinions, and supporting plans and intentions.
2. It adds weight to the things that people 'know' but perhaps don't 'do' (or do as much of).
3. It discredits any unproven received wisdom that is contradictory.

Most usefully, the report contains a very user-friendly article as Appendix 1. This is entitled 'Five "no-brainers" from neuroscience research' and is written by Dr Paul Howard-Jones, reader in neuroscience and education at the University of Bristol. He begins by making a point that is very valid to all leaders and many followers. The brain is plastic; it changes, like a muscle, the more you exercise specific parts of it the more those parts grow. He demonstrates this by mentioning that there is a direct correlation between the size of the brain region critical to navigation and the number of years the brain's owner has been a London cabbie.

For readers unfamiliar with the rules concerning London's black cab drivers, they are not allowed to refer to sat-nav or maps, but must take and pass a practical course and exam in memory navigation of the whole London area.

Similarly, trainee jugglers show increases in the relevant areas of their brains after as little as three months of training in the art of juggling.

Here is a short summary of the five no-brainer points:

1. **Improve creativity two ways:** First, working independently can be detrimental; the brain concentrates on the matter in hand by reducing its activity in automatic thinking processes. This can help solve the problem but it can also lead to a mental block or a fixation with a particular solution. Interacting with others opens up the automatic thinking processes and can help shift a mental block. Second, the brain responds

creatively to unusual challenges. For example, in adult brains the straightforward challenge to create a story produced less activity in the brain than the challenge to create a story incorporating a list of unrelated words.

2. **Improve learning by spacing it out in shorter chunks:** Received wisdom has suggested that 'little but often' improves people's capacity to learn... neuroscience has now told us why. We do more internal 'verbal rehearsal' in the down-time between learning sessions, and this reinforces what we have learned by repetition. This works not only for rote learning of facts but also learning sequences such as mathematics and grammar.

3. **Improve your memory by getting a good night's sleep:** When you sleep well your brain unconsciously reflects on the experience of the day; this reflection is, once again, a form of reinforcement, committing our experience to memory. If the experience was intentionally 'learning', clearly the sleep helps. If not, it is still a good idea to be able to remember what happened at work yesterday!

4. **Technology can be a double-edged sword:** Relaxing ten feet in front of the TV before bedtime helps release the sleep-inducing melatonin. Working (or playing) at a bright computer screen 20 inches away delays the natural release, resulting in poorer sleep (see point 3 above). On the other hand there is evidence that some off-the-shelf action games can help people to improve visual attention and avoid visual distraction. (For example, laparoscopic surgeons who play video games make significantly fewer errors than ones who don't.)

5. **Get off your butt if you want your brain to work better:** Both in the short term and long term, exercise increases blood flow to the brain and improves brain function. In one experiment 2 × 3-minute sprints improved people's memory function by 20 per cent in an immediate test. In the longer term, the brains of physically fit people usually have a larger hippocampus than for unfit people; the size of the hippocampus is directly related to memory.

A final little useful element of the report is a condensed (also 5-point) tip list from the survey participants. It relates very much to 'brain-friendly learning', but since you want to learn from every experience you have (and as a leader you want your people to do likewise) it is included here.

Five brain-friendly techniques recommended by the survey contributors

Find and give time and encourage active reflection.

When providing information, do it in short bursts; 10 to 15 minutes rather than three-hour presentations.

Introduce physical movement into the day; even if it is just a walk around the block.

Introduce opportunities for people to find things out for themselves, rather than spoon-feeding them.

Try to bring some emotion into the messages: shock or laughter are proven to make messages far more memorable than the grey 'corporate' language and images of a staid organization.

So what are the big takeaways here?

- Ask your (-self and your) people every day to reflect on what they have learned in their experience today.
- Try avoiding giving your opinion on things and ask your people for their ideas.
- Remember that your brain is more powerful than your computer... switch the PC/Mac/tablet/smartphone off and just think!

Source

www.cipd.co.uk/hr-resources/research/neuroscience-learning.aspx

See also

Chapter 13 – To be (here) or not to be (here), that is the question

Chapter 18 – Leadership and leaders; let's get complex

Chapter 26 – Learning; it's a generational thing

Chapter 40 – You can NOT be serious!

15 SUCCESSFUL CHANGE BEGINS WITH 'GOOD' COMMUNICATION

Many organizations and leaders are secretive about change until ready to make it... this is the reason many changes fail!

Change is inevitable; no organization can stand still and expect to survive.

There are many pressures on a leader when initiating and driving through a change programme:

- A commercial need for confidentiality
- A reluctance to 'wash the organization's dirty linen in public'
- The sheer size of the organization (or the geographic spread of its constituent parts)
- A reluctance to openly say 'we need to change but I don't know what or how'.

As a result, many senior executives will create a small team to help them plan and manage the change. This team may include experts specifically drafted in, external specialist consultants and other senior managers. They operate on a 'need to know' basis until they have come up with their plan. Only then are they comfortable in sharing it with the rest of the organization.

In 2002, Mercer Human Resources and the International Association of Business Communicators conducted a major survey regarding change practices around the globe. They sought opinions from 12,000 people from a wide range of organizations and at a wide range of levels of seniority. They then sampled senior executives from Fortune 200 companies to get a different perspective. Then, based on their findings to date, they interviewed 250 communications executives to identify what were the best and worst change management practices.

Their findings suggest that the most effective and successful change initiatives benefit from a very different approach.

The top five WORST change practices were:

1. Failing to communicate to all employees about change
2. Not articulating change vision/objectives rationale
3. Being dishonest about change processes and implications
4. Not giving employees a voice in the change process
5. Failing to plan for change.

Number 1 clearly suggests that the small dedicated change management team approach, operating on a need-to-know basis, is divisive.

Number 2 clearly suggests that if people don't understand 'why' a change is necessary they are less likely to support it; usually, senior management understands why a change is necessary and what it is aiming to achieve but all too often this is considered either too complex for the masses or simply that 'theirs is not to reason why'.

In number 3 'dishonest' not only means actively lying about implications but also *hiding* the implications or not telling people until 'the time is right'.

Number 4 is a double whammy: not only do people feel resentful that they were not consulted, but also the lost opportunity to avoid the later flood of 'I could have told you that wouldn't work because...' comments.

Number 5 probably doesn't need any further comment... except to say that trying to avoid it may result in closeting yourself away with a team of experts and producing a splendid plan that completely falls into the traps of numbers 1 to 4.

The top five BEST change practices were:

1. Effective communication
2. Employee involvement or buy-in
3. Leadership and commitment from senior management
4. Evidence that management is 'living the change'
5. Explicit business imperative for the change.

In Number 1 'effective' covers the timing of communication as well as the content of the messages. It also covers the media delivery method – but more of that later.

Number 2 clearly suggests that the 'small team of specialists' approach needs to engage in a lot of consultation with the workforce (not just their trade union). It also links to the matter of effective communication: simply giving people information doesn't get their involvement and buy-in, you have to get information back from them. Communication is a two-way process.

Number 3 has another big message for the 'small team of specialists' approach: senior management cannot simply brief a team and leave it to get on with it. The leadership has to be involved with the change programme on a day-to-day basis and not continue their own operations as if it were business as usual.

Number 4 is dependent upon the type of change being initiated. If the change is cultural or behavioural this is fairly straightforward. Management simply has to identify the new culture or behaviours that are needed and do them themselves and manage in a way that encourages and creates role models.

Where the changes being brought in only really affect the 'rank and file', it is more challenging for managers to demonstrate that they are also 'living the change'. What needs to be done will depend on the circumstances, suffice it to say that if managers are aware that they need to be seen to 'live the change', then most will be able to work out how to with regard to the specific situation they find themselves in.

In Number 5 the most important word is 'explicit'. Organizations instigate change for any number of reasons, for instance:

- to comply with new legal regulations
- to fight competitors
- because the economy has shrunk and their market is disappearing
- to respond to new technology
- to reduce cost and waste thus increasing efficiency
- to catch up with smaller changes that should have been made in the past
- to continually improve
- to prepare for an expected change in their market
- in response to customer demand
- to absorb or be absorbed after a merger or acquisition.

Whatever the reason it must be made clear to everyone and then be repeated often. This avoids the old joke:

'When you are up to your arse in alligators it is difficult to remember that the initial aim was to drain the swamp.'

Bonus observation from the author's own experience

I have a lot of experience working with the public sector in the UK, be that central government, local authorities or quangos. One of the constant comments I hear from public sector employees is that the changes foisted upon them are changes that are made simply because a different political party is now in government.

I also do a lot of work in the commercial and not-for-profit sectors and have heard many stories of change programmes that were initiated from the top simply because they were following a 'fad' or fashion. Sometimes that fad was related to new technology or software that was seen to be cutting edge, and sometimes it was to do with the latest management culture/style theory.

In neither of these situations is there a clear 'business imperative' for the change... they *appear* to be initiated on a whim.

A change in government may well result in major changes for the public servants in their administration, and the mandate of the people is the business case.

Adopting a cutting-edge technology or a new management style requires a detailed analysis of the benefits that it will bring... this then becomes the business case for change.

Media for communicating change

The study also looked at the media for communicating change to the workforce. It looked at two aspects of this: availability and value. The results are below:

Media	Availability	Value
a. Individual meeting between manager and staff member	89%	76%
b. Departmental/team meetings between manager and staff	90%	67%
c. Email or other ICT	95%	65%
d. Leadership presentations to staff	82%	45%
e. Organization's newsletter	90%	32%
f. Information packs/brochures	81%	27%
g. Information helpline	51%	22%
h. Employee grapevine/rumours	98%	19%
i. Video	66%	14%
j. Bulletin boards	80%	12%

Particular points to note with regard to the medium or channel of communications are:

d) leadership giving a formal presentation is less than 50 per cent effective as a demonstration of the critically important need to show commitment to the change. Leadership producing a video is even less effective.

f), g) and i) are all very commonly used but all very low on effectiveness.

c) is perhaps surprisingly successful; predominantly due to their speed and perhaps the fact that they are two-way communications since people can respond with a question or challenge.

a) and b) though possibly the most time consuming, and reliant on the individual manager's communication skills, remain the most effective way of preventing change from failing.

So what are the big takeaways here?

- **Start engaging with your people NOW.** Don't wait until you have a change programme in the offing. Tell them the strategies of the organization and explain why these are the strategies; that way, when you need to explain a business imperative for change they will be used to understanding the bigger picture.
- **Instigate a regular meeting with your people to ask them what changes they'd like to propose.** What change is your workplace screaming out for? Are you completely happy with the following six characteristics of the organization. Use the SCREAM mnemonic:

  - Staff: the number of people, their locations and job descriptions, the way they are organized and where they are located. This can also extend to include whether you have got the right people in the first place!
  - Culture: this is the general culture that we have in the workplace. Are we autocratic or consultative, are we militant or pacifist?
  - Resources that you have to work with: this can range from the tools to consumables, from the computers to the workwear.
  - Environment in which you work: everything from the cleanliness and tidiness to the lighting, heating and ventilation.
  - Abilities of the people: does everyone have all the skills and knowledge that you'd like them to have in order to do the job well and keep them and you happy?
  - Methods (both the ones that each person uses and the overall method that connects it all together).

- **Remember that communication is the key to successful change.**

See also

Chapter 1 – Spreadsheets alone do not a judgement make

Chapter 4 – I read it, but what the heck did it mean?

Chapter 28 – What happens when you (or someone you manage) make decisions under pressure?

Chapter 37 – 'Science, schmience' ... take it with a pinch of salt

Chapter 38 – Learning from successful change

16 GETTING ENGAGED MEANS COMMITTING AND STAYING THE COURSE

An engaged workforce isn't something that is fluffy and nice-to-have-when-you-can-afford-it. It is a strategy for success

The Corporate Leadership Council is a global membership organization that exists to give scientific rigour to management development. It publishes around 200 studies per annum with the aim of 'helping business leaders evaluate new issues and challenges'.

In 2004 it published a major study into the topic of employee engagement. The report begins by pointing out that there are differing definitions of what actually constitutes 'engagement' and so to provide clarity they laid down their own definition for the purposes of the study.

Engagement is the extent to which employees commit to something or someone in their organization and how hard they work and how long they stay as a result of that commitment.

The sample group for the study was significant:

* more than 50,000 people
* from 59 different organizations
* in 30 countries
* across 14 industries
* 54 per cent male and 46 per cent female
* the full range of working age, from 18-year-olds to 60+

- tenure ranging from new starters to employees with 31+ years of service
- across virtually all work functions and positions in the organizational hierarchy.

> It is valuable to note that the terminology of the report refers to 'employees'... this includes not just shop-floor staff but also supervisors, managers, senior managers and even the leadership team themselves; although 68 per cent of respondents were non-managerial, the remainder represented up to and including VPs and senior executives.

The study categorized two types of commitment:

Rational commitment: The extent to which an employee judged the benefits to their own self-interest – be they financial, developmental or professional.

Emotional commitment: The extent to which the employee valued, enjoyed and believed in their work, their manager, their co-workers and their organization.

(As you can see, the study looked at four 'focal points' for commitment: work, colleagues, manager and organization.)

The study measured two 'outputs' of commitment:

- **Discretionary effort:** an employee's willingness to go beyond their job description by helping co-workers, taking on extra responsibilities and proactively developing themselves and working practices.
- **Intent to stay:** their desire to remain with their current employer based upon whether they intended to start looking for a new job within a year, whether they frequently considered handing in their notice, or whether they were already looking for another job.

The respondents' answers ranged across the bell curve for commitment:

- 11 per cent were **true believers**. These people demonstrated a high level of commitment to their work, their colleagues, their manager and the organization. They were high performers who regularly assisted colleagues, volunteered for extra duties and looked for ways to do their jobs better.
- 76 per cent were **agnostics**. This group comprised pretty good performers who neither went out of their way nor shirked. Their intentions to stay ranged widely. They showed a high level of commitment (emotional or rational) to one of the focal points but had only moderate levels of commitment to other elements.
- 13 per cent were **highly uncommitted**. This cadre comprised poor performers who frequently put in just enough effort to get by. They were four times more likely to desert the organization than the agnostic employee and nine times more likely than the true believers.

The report runs to some 45 pages, so here is a précis of some of the more interesting of its discoveries.

1. Demographic generalizations and received wisdoms aren't always right. For instance, the belief that younger people have little commitment. The differential between the under-40s and the over-40s as a percentage of the most committed employees are 10.6 per cent and 11.7 per cent respectively. Similarly, the difference between parents and non-parents is very low; the percentage of the most committed is 10.8 per cent and 11.4 per cent respectively.
2. The differences between organizations were enormous! The percentage of an organization's workforce that ranked in the 'true believer' category ranged from 23.8 per cent of the population in the 'best' organization to a derisory 2.9 per cent in the 'worst'.
3. While engagement was significant to the overall rates of observable performance improvement it was not the only factor; 40 per cent of performance improvement could be

linked to employee engagement and a remaining 57 per cent was actually down to 'direct performance inflectors'... these include job relevant information, on-the-job development and having the right resources.

4. 10:6:2 ratio... a 10 per cent improvement in a person's commitment results in a 6 per cent improvement in the discretionary effort they put in. A 6 per cent improvement in effort produces a 2 per cent improvement in performance.

5. 10:9 ratio... a 10 per cent improvement in commitment results in a 9 per cent reduction in the likelihood that an employee will leave. (When you consider the cost of recruiting and inducting a new employee you can see the value in retaining people, especially once they are committed to the organization.)

6. 71 per cent of companies with above-average employee engagement did better in terms of 12-month revenue growth relative to their specific industry competitors. 62 per cent of companies with below-average employee engagement scored worse than their competitors.

7. It wasn't the rational commitment that had the most effect on employees' efforts, but the emotional commitment. A strong emotional commitment to the organization resulted in a 43.2 per cent higher level of discretionary effort... whereas a strong rational commitment to the organization only resulted in an 18.4 per cent higher level of discretionary effort. Similar differences were found for the commitment to team and manager.

8. Conversely, a strong rational commitment to the organization results in the highest improvement in intent to stay, though emotional commitment is still strong in the retention arena.

9. Very interestingly for senior executives are the effects that their behaviours have on their people's discretionary effort. Demonstrating that you:

- are open to new ideas
- care deeply about employees
- make employee development a priority
- are committed to creating new jobs.

Creates a greater amount of discretionary effort from your people than any of the more commonly seen traits of leading and managing people, selecting and implementing strategy, or your day-to-day process management ability.

The study went on to identify the 'levers' on engagement; those elements that organizational managers can use to improve employee engagement at all levels.

The study identified more than 300 different levers and the report lists the top 160 of these. Interestingly for all aspiring and incumbent leaders and managers, the report identified that almost every action a manager takes has an effect on discretionary effort. The report lists more than 40 day-to-day management actions and characteristics that have an impact in excess of 20 per cent. They include (among others):

• Commits to diversity
• Demonstrates honesty and integrity
• Adapts to changing circumstances
• Clearly articulates organizational goals
• Sets realistic performance expectations
• Accurately appraises employee performance
• Defends direct reports
• Trusts employees to do their job
• Listens carefully to views and opinions
• Holds people accountable
• Articulates the long-term vision for the future.

The report also provides a handy guide to the top 50 'most effective levers of engagement'. Bearing in mind that more than 60 per cent of the respondents were from non-managerial grades the top two are very interesting. They are 1) Connection between the individual's day-to-day work and the overall strategy of the organization; and 2) the importance of my job to organizational success.

So, when was the last time you discussed these elements with the individuals in your team?

So what are the big takeaways here?

- Spread the word that employee engagement isn't just a nice-to-have-when-we-can-afford-it. It is a genuine contributor to bottom-line productivity and efficiency.
- Get hold of a copy of the report and assess your organization or team to see what you are doing to exploit the different levers.
- Remember that a large number of the levers of engagement are related to the individual actions of members of the management... in other words, YOU!

Source

www.usc.edu/programs/cwfl/assets/pdf/Employee%20 engagement.pdf

See also

Chapter 18 – Leadership and leaders; let's get complex

Chapter 21 – Management and leadership... a hot topic! But for whom?

Chapter 29 – Is getting engaged really worth the effort?

Chapter 33 – Find out what your followers think about you, and talk to them about it!

Chapter 35 – 'Trust me, I'm a manager'

17 SPARTAN OR 'HOUSE AND GARDEN'?

Should a workplace be solely functional or are plants and artwork beneficial to productivity?

Health and safety demands the removal of unnecessary and potentially dangerous clutter (even if H&S doesn't actually demand it, it is often cited as the rationale for clearing non-organizational items from the workplace).

Equality consideration removed the girly calendars and smutty cartoons of yesteryear... and in many workplaces a zero-tolerance approach means that nothing is allowed on the walls.

When organizations are laying-off staff and cutting operations back to the essentials it is seen as wasteful to spend money on frivolities such as office plants, artwork and nice decor.

The received wisdom for most industries is that in order to maximize productivity workspaces should be clear of clutter, functional and 'lean'. This approach was initially espoused by Josiah Wedgwood in the 18th century and Frederick Taylor then reiterated the concept in his theories of scientific management, and the lean movement in the late 20th century has reinforced it further.

The intuitive nature of the lean workplace theory is, however, seldom backed up with any genuine proof of its genuineness... it is simply seen as 'common sense'.

Various studies have been carried out over the years that look at the enrichment of office space and the effects on both the *actual* working environment and the workforce's perceptions. For instance, plants in the workplace can have measured effects on air quality *and* psychological effects on people's perceptions of air quality.

In 2014, Marlon Nieuwenhuis, of Cardiff University in Wales, led a study with three colleagues from other UK, Australian and Dutch universities – Tom Postmes, University of Groningen, Craig Knight, University of Exeter, and Alexander Haslam, University of Queensland. Their work was different to the previous studies in that it focused solely on the provision of plants and it measured productivity as well as the workforce's environment.

Their study used real commercial offices of a functioning business. The methodology was to take a single, large open-plan office floor and divide it into two separate areas, one to be landscaped with plants and one to remain stripped and purely functional. This removed differentiations of lights, accessibility and location as well as providing 'before and after' comparisons.

The study ran in three phases:

1. Environmental satisfaction: measuring the workforce's perceptions of a) the air quality; b) ability to concentrate; c) satisfaction; and d) productivity.
2. The same areas of measurement but with two differences. a) more objective methods of measuring productivity rather than subjective perception; and b) an extended timeframe.
3. Purely a measure of productivity.

Study 1 took place in London in the hot-desking offices of a consultancy company. The staff were very well paid and operated with a high degree of professional autonomy. They could choose where in the office they worked. A survey was carried out before the greening of the study area and then again two weeks afterwards. In comparison to the people who worked in the lean area, the people who worked in the green area reported that the air quality was better, they were able to concentrate more effectively and after three weeks their productivity was enhanced.

One surprise was that the staff working in the lean area reported a similar rise in their level of satisfaction with the work environment. (It was surmised that though the planting wasn't immediately in the lean area the staff working there passed through and saw the landscaping during their working day, which suggests that greening the common areas as well as the discrete workstations is worthy of consideration.)

Study 2 took place in the Netherlands in a financial services company's contact centre. To counter the surprise effect mentioned above, in this study the team used two different floors of the same building. The staff here were less well paid and in a more hierarchical structure. Their productivity is already measured in terms of call duration, time they put the caller on hold and the time taken to complete post call records. Surveys were carried out and productivity measured before the study started, two weeks in, and three and a half months in.

Again the green area staff reported higher perceptions of air quality and satisfaction than the people working in the spartan area, and this was common in the short- and longer-term surveys. There was a marginal difference in the reported level of concentration between green and spartan. The surprise was that in spite of staff perceptions being improved by the greening of their workspace, the objective measure of productivity showed no difference. This potentially calls into question the bottom-line short-term value of greening the office but the measurement does need to be considered; call duration is widely used as a measure of call centre agent productivity but it measures efficiency rather than quality. There are many reasons why a call may be short and only one of them is that the customer has received a high level of service.

Study 3. In the light of the outcome of the productivity measures in Study 2, Study 3 moved to a more rigorous and objective 'laboratory-style' measurement of productivity. The study took place in London in the offices of a professional service company. Participants were briefed and randomly allocated a workstation in either the lean or green space. The two spaces were laid out identically and provided with identical furniture and equipment. The green space was also fitted out with large plants and every participant in this area could see at least three from their desk.

Participants were asked to evaluate their workspace prior to starting the three time-pressured tasks; information management, information processing and vigilance.

- Information management was tested by sorting a shuffled stack for company memoranda into chronological order against the clock.
- Information processing was tested by completing a multiple-choice quiz on the content of the memoranda, again against the clock.
- Vigilance was tested by timed 'proofreading' of a document and extracting information from it.

The outcomes of the study were conclusive: a green workspace was more appreciated by employees; they were faster in their work and with no increase in the rate of errors.

The overall study provides a clear debunking of the myth that 'lean and mean' is beneficial to productivity. Making a workplace 'a green and pleasant land', rather than 'a dark Satanic mill', not only makes people happier but it also makes them more productive; they work more quickly, they can concentrate for longer and they exhibit high levels of accuracy and quality.

So what are the big takeaways here?

- **Spread the word**; tell people, especially the people who hold the purse strings, about this research. Pot plants aren't just pretty, they actively contribute to the bottom line.
- **Encourage people to bring plants into work and have them on their desks.** (Bonus observation from the author: one of my clients has a small basement room in their office building. It has no windows and no natural light, it is quite cramped and the actual air quality is nothing to write home about but it is one of the most popular meeting rooms in the building. The walls are decorated with a giant photo-mural of a forest; it isn't a landscape just green trees in dappled sunlight... perhaps even pictures of plants are beneficial to our perception of wellbeing!)

- **Remember the power of plants**; if you need to boost productivity in a particularly difficult time, consider 'decking the halls with boughs' rather than 'clearing the decks for action'.

Source

Nieuwenhuis, M., Knight, C., Postmes, T. & Haslam, S. A. (2014), 'The Relative Benefits of Green versus Lean Office Space: Three Field Experiments', *Journal of Experimental Psychology*, Vol. 20 Issue 3 pp 199–214

See also

Chapter 5 – 'Workers' play time' – is it really worth it?

Chapter 7 – 'An employee's workspace is his castle... or should be!'

Chapter 11 – To follow me they have to be able to see me, right?

18 LEADERSHIP AND LEADERS; LET'S GET COMPLEX

Leadership isn't simply a matter of getting people to follow you... it is also about having the wisdom and capacity to balance your style

Over the years the debate about 'what is leadership' and what makes a good leader has carried on and on... Mary Uhl-Bien, Russ Marion and Bill McKelvey published an article in January 2007 to propose a new approach.

The content of that article is included in this book not because their approach is based on a new study, but because their approach is so heavily referenced to other works. The whole article is 22 pages in length and nearly 4 pages of that is taken up with references to other scholarly studies. It could be referred to as 'How to Become Ridiculously Well Read on Leadership Theory in One Easy Lesson'.

The premise of their article is that most leadership models and theory are based upon what succeeds in an industrial age. It is generally top-down and is excellently suited to a production economy where control and centralized goals are critical to success. Our world economy is no longer predominantly production based; we live more in the 'knowledge era' and a different paradigm is appropriate to leadership and leaders.

In the knowledge age and in knowledge-based organizations the need is for more informal networks of individuals sharing expertise and driving towards the rapidly shifting objectives, whereas in the production/industrial age the need was more for alignment, standardization, control and homogeneity.

They propose a new model, which they call Complexity Leadership Theory. In this they draw a difference between 'leaders' (as in the people recognized in a hierarchy as having the formal authority) and 'leadership' (as in a series of functions that bring about success). To quote from the report:

Much of leadership thinking has failed to recognize that leadership is not merely the influential act of an individual or individuals but rather is embedded in a complex interplay of numerous interacting forces.

Complexity Leadership Theory defines three leadership functions: adaptive leadership, administrative leadership and enabling leadership.

Adaptive leadership

This is the dynamic that arises through people's interactions when they adjust to, and cope with, tensions and problems.

It is not an act of authority and it happens throughout the organization.

It appears when interdependent individuals or groups are competing over differences in ideas, needs and preferences.

It results in:

- alliances of people and groups
- development of new ideas
- solutions and outcomes.

It is the catalyst for most change in the organization; an example of adaptive leadership might be when two parties with opposed opinions are engaged in a debate over relative merits and suddenly one or both generates a new understanding of the situation.

This is often referred to as an 'a-ha' moment.

'A-ha' solutions cannot realistically be claimed by any one individual; they are the product of tensions between different opinions and therefore one will only happen when the interaction takes place.

Adaptive leadership is really only recognized when the outcome has *significance* and *impact*:

- Significance is the practical usefulness of the outcome. This can be measured in revenue, efficiency, cost saving or effectiveness.
- Impact is the level to which the outcome is embraced by people other than the group who gave it birth.

Impact can be completely independent of significance as it can be directly affected by the rank or reputation of the 'parents' *and* the imaginations of other people; most of us are aware of insignificant ideas having a major impact due to the authority of the originator. Conversely, we probably all know of instances where brilliant ideas had virtually no impact simply because they were not circulated. This can also be directly attributed to the level to which 'administrative leadership' is exercised.

Administrative leadership

This is the series of activities by individuals (or groups of individuals) where they plan and organize actions to result in an efficient manner. Administrative leadership builds vision, structures tasks, allocates resources, defines strategies, and manages crises and conflicts.

Administrative leadership is almost always a top-down function based upon authority and position. It has the power to make decisions, and this is an area where:

an excess of administrative leadership can stifle people's capacity to change, evolve and develop new ideas.

The authors are clear that administrative leadership is still appropriate to support a performance management culture and situations where accountability and compliance are business critical.

Enabling leadership

Enabling leadership is twofold:

1. It is the creation of the environment and the conditions where adaptive leadership can occur.

2. It is the effective balancing of the control and certainty of administrative leadership and the freedom and conflict of adaptive leadership.

Enabling leadership behaviours can happen anywhere though middle managers are often most ideally placed to exhibit them. Three things that enabling leadership does to foster adaptive leadership (and thus innovation) are:

- to foster and encourage interaction between different individuals and groups
- to highlight and underline mutual benefit to these parties
- to inject some creative tension, motivate and coordinate action.

Enabling leadership can also affect the impact of adaptive leadership by disseminating the innovative 'a-ha' outcomes throughout the organization.

Enabling leaders demonstrate personal commitment to the idea, promote the idea through informal networks and willingly risk their position and reputation to ensure its success.

Reading the article is quite hard going, since it is scattered with references to other people's work, academic jargon and long words. Wading through its 22 pages is not for the fainthearted. However, once you can get the gist of it, it is in itself an 'a-ha' moment; it all makes perfect sense and clearly paints a very useful model for leadership in a knowledge economy.

So what are the big takeaways here?

- **If you work in any environment other than a production one,** question the concept that traditional leadership will take your organization through the next decade successfully.
- **When you are looking to promote or recruit,** look for people's enabling leadership skills as well as their administrative leadership ability – regardless of whether they will be taking on a formal management role.
- **When one of your team brings you a problem, remember this particular line:** 'A major function of leaders has historically

been to solve problems, to intervene when dilemmas arise or when individuals differ on task-related activities. Such action, however, can stifle interdependency and limit adaptive mechanisms.'

Source

Uhl-Bien, M., Marion, R. & McKelvey, B. (2007), 'Complexity Leadership Theory: Shifting leadership from the industrial age to the knowledge era'. *The Leadership Quarterly*, Vol. 18 Issue 4 pp 298–318
www.sciencedirect.com/science/article/pii/S1048984307000689

See also

Chapter 6 – As a leader, it is a matter of priorities

Chapter 16 – Getting engaged means committing and staying the course

Chapter 29 – Is getting engaged really worth the effort?

Chapter 34 – Talent management – have you got your EVP right?

19 THE CUSTOMER IS ALWAYS RIGHT... WRONG!

When it comes to customer complaints, prevention can be better than cure... and far less expensive in the long run

We've all heard the old adage that the customer is always right and we all know that it is more observed in spirit than in reality. Most organizations measure the number of complaints that they receive from customers but often they don't actually analyse the underlying reasons for the complaints.

TARP (Technical Assistance Research Programs) was the name of a US organization that championed data collection and analysis in the field of customer satisfaction. We say 'was' because although the organization goes from strength to strength it has changed its name to CX Act.

In 2001 the then president of TARP, John Goodman, unveiled the results of a major survey into customer complaints, the underlying causes for the dissatisfaction and some case studies to demonstrate how organizations had radically reduced customer dissatisfaction in innovative ways.

In large part his objective was to turn organizations' strategies from 'complaint management' to 'complaint prevention' through a scientific analysis of their current complaints.

Since the causes of customer complaints vary – depending on factors such as the nature of the product or service, the price and the industry sector – Goodman presented the causes simply in categories rather than in a ranked order of magnitude. The categories were common across industries:

a. Defects caused by production or service failure or employee error	b. Marketing overpromises	c. Misleading marketing	d. Customer error that is a reasonable mistake	e. Customer 'stupidity' or unreasonable customer expectation

Goodman's contention was that only the first category could be addressed by the production/operations or the customer service function. The others required a more holistic effort to rectify.

More importantly, TARP was making the point that with intelligent effort on a holistic basis, many issues could be *prevented* from recurring (i.e. they could be pre-empted with future customers). Obviously with a little foresight this could be taken a stage further and many could be foreseen and therefore prevented altogether in the future.

Simple quality checks, good recruitment and training, and effective performance management should reduce **defects** to minimal levels. This is fairly self-evident and most organizations, large and small, already make significant efforts to achieve this.

Marketing overpromises and deliberately **misleading marketing** are, clearly, predominantly the remit of the marketing and sales departments. More recent situations in most developed nations suggest that this is still a widespread problem. Consistent lawsuits and government-mandated compensation campaigns on the grounds of mis-selling are costing businesses dearly. HomeServe was fined £30.6 million for mis-selling emergency cover insurance. Banks have faced massive costs over PPI claims. Energy company tariffs have been heavily criticized. Solar panel sales are under scrutiny. Many companies have now recognized the danger of financial incentivization of their sales force, especially for these high-value items.

Complaints that arise due to **customers making a reasonable mistake** is almost always preventable. Goodman referred to a flooring manufacturer/installer who received a number of complaints that their new flooring was failing. They rapidly discovered that customers were continuing to clean their new flooring using the same cleaning products that they had always used. This was unnecessary and was the cause of the damage, but the customers were unaware that the new flooring didn't need, and was in fact damaged by, the abrasive nature of the old cleaners. The company immediately embarked on a contact programme with all their customers. They rang each one and spent a few minutes explaining the change; this eliminated the problem almost immediately *and* presented the image to the customers of a caring and considerate supplier.

Goodman went on to reinforce this particular case study with another from Alamo Rent A Car. Alamo produced a small, inexpensive 'educational' pamphlet entitled 'The Consumer's Guide to Renting a Car'. They mailed this out to 2,000 of their customers. They then surveyed this group and a control group of 2,000 other customers to whom they had not sent the guide. The survey showed two important outcomes:

- customers who received the guide and then rented a car were 24 per cent more satisfied than those who didn't receive the guide before they rented.
- the group who received the guide were 15 per cent more likely to rent from Alamo next time than the group who didn't get sent a guide.

Alamo also measured the incidence of problems for the two groups of customers in their post-guide rental period. The number of calls from guide recipients remained almost identical to the non-guide renters BUT the difference was the outcome of the calls. The guided customers' calls resulted in significantly fewer and less costly (to Alamo) bills.

While sending out pamphlets has a not insignificant cost, this sort of education of customers can also be done more simply by labelling. Dannon/Danone makes and sells cherry yoghurt. Cherries have hard stones and ensuring that all stones are removed without reducing the fruit to a liquid is a very costly business. Danone overcomes the potential for problems by labelling the individual pots with a warning that they may contain stones. When the labelling was removed, the number of complaints doubled. When the label was reinstated, the number of complaints halved.

Goodman's final category was **customer stupidity** or **unreasonable expectation**. To demonstrate this Goodman quoted several complaints received by a manufacturer of domestic bleach. The customers were complaining about the unpleasant taste of the product; they were using it to try to whiten their teeth! Clearly there is little that can be done to completely eradicate complaints borne of customer idiocy, but if you ever have to call a software or hardware supplier to seek assistance you will note that nowadays one of the early questions you are asked is: 'Is the computer switched on?'. It may appear that the help desk is insulting your intelligence but the reality is that some customers have proven to be that ignorant.

OK, there are the survey findings, what can you do with them?

The first message is that it is really important to identify root causes of problems and complaints, even if your customers are internal. Do this either as a specific project or simply by making notes of the issues over a period. Sort the root causes into categories along the lines of those Goodman identified.

Once you have identified the causes, decide who in the organization you need to involve in the solution; you may be able to simply put a plan into practice with your own team, alternatively you may need to get the marketing or packaging departments involved. If you *genuinely* believe that customer stupidity is a significant contributor to your problems, it is probably worth considering whether there is anything you can do to mitigate the issue.

Many organizations are already at this stage so you need not fear being laughed at; sets of carving knives are available that are clearly labelled as not suitable for children under 36 months, cough mixture for the under-5s carries a warning not to operate heavy machinery after taking a dose, fruit-flavoured soaps and shampoos tell their customer that they are not foodstuffs, and inflatable pool toys in the shape of crocodiles warn us that they are not lifesaving equipment. Most of these warnings are a direct or indirect result of the TARP survey.

So what are the big takeaways here?

- **Next time someone in your team is exasperated about having to deal with a complaint,** ask them to analyse the root cause; then they (or you) will be in a position to prevent it happening again.
- **Take the time to proactively assess the causes of problems and complaints.** Once you know the causes, you can sensibly prioritize your responses.
- **Remember that though you cannot legislate against stupidity** you may well be able to mitigate the effects it could bring.

Source

www.customerservicegroup.com/pdf/csn1210docs.pdf

See also

Chapter 1 – Spreadsheets alone do not a judgement make

Chapter 4 – I read it, but what the heck did it mean?

Chapter 35 – 'Trust me, I'm a manager'

20 IT SOUNDS SCIENTIFIC AND OBJECTIVE, BUT IS IT SCIENCE?

There can be 'good' science and 'bad' science or good science used badly. The magic is in knowing which you are looking at!

You are looking to recruit a new person to your team. The role is going to be business critical. You want to get it right first time. You decide to take a more objective and professional approach than just: 'I'll recognize good when I see it.' You draw up a job description and a person specification and you discuss these with the team members to get a sense check. All going well so far...

Next you go to get a bit of best practice advice from the HR function and they suggest that to make it really scientific and objective (and to avoid accusations of bias or unfair discrimination) you have all the applicants undertake a psychometric test.

Technically speaking these sorts of instruments are actually 'assessments' not 'tests'... you can't fail them, they simply assess you not test you. However, the common parlance is 'test' so we'll use that term.

They suggest a Myers-Briggs Type Indicator or MBTI. This is a widely used assessment tool; McKinsey and Co. uses it, General Motors uses it. In fact, so many organizations use it that two and a half million tests are administered every year and the owners are rumoured to generate more than US$20 million per annum from it. It has been around since 1943, so it isn't exactly a flash-in-the-pan, fad/fashion tool either; it's proven.

The test requires a person to complete a questionnaire of 93 questions that analyses four different areas of personal preference:

1. Decision-making – are you a logical and objective decision-maker or a values-driven decision-maker?
2. Inward/outward focus – are you the 'life-and-soul' or the quiet contemplative type?
3. Information absorption – are you a purely facts-based person or more of a visionary?
4. Your 'outward' life preferences – are you a careful planner or a seat of the pants maverick?

(For brevity, I've paraphrased the alternatives in the descriptions above.)

In each of the four areas there are two opposed alternatives, so any one person will be categorized into one of 16 categories. Each category is known, like the MBTI itself by a four letter acronym.

The theory is that you, as the manager can aim to replace a leaver with a person of similar personality. Or you could be looking to recruit someone with complementary personal traits. Or you may have identified that a particular type is successful in this role and wish to use the test to look for aptitude.

Great! This takes the guesswork out of it. It gives you confidence in your decision. Or it saves you from making a major and very embarrassing error. What a brilliant tool!

But is it?

Even the owners have said that it shouldn't be used for recruitment and selection purposes.

Others are sceptical of its value as a scientific test at all.

So what is fundamentally wrong with the MBTI?

The premise is that personality is a constant and that therefore once you have been assessed as being of a particular personality type this type will remain with you always. While leopards may not change their spots, is the MBTI a reliable way of identifying a person's personality type?

Scientific studies have been carried out to simply test and retest the same people to see whether they get the same results when they take the test. As long ago as 1979, Howes and Carskadon carried out a study with a five-week gap between the test and the retest; they found that up to 50 per cent of people got a different result the second time.

There have been a number of studies that have looked to identify the reasons for these changes; they have identified a number of areas of concern relating to the statistical machinations of the test results and the 'binary' nature of the categorizations (if you scored 100 out of 200 you'd be in one category but if you scored 105 out of 200 you'd be in a different category; it is black or white with no shades of grey). Suffice to say that, regardless of the underlying reasons, if the test is not reliable over a short five-week period we need to be rather reticent about using it to make such lifelong decisions as career path, recruitment or promotions.

The reason why MBTI is so widespread and popular with its champions remains untested, but perhaps there are three main reasons. The first is that 'if it's good enough for General Motors then it is good for everyone'. So many big reputable organizations use it that people don't necessarily question it. Second, the people in these organizations who administer it have spent a not-inconsiderable licence sum to do so; people who've paid a lot of money for something seldom want to damage their own credibility by accepting it was a lemon! And, finally, the results are always quite flattering... looking at the first words of each of the 16 categories you are:

- Responsible
- Warm
- Idealistic
- Innovative

- Action oriented
- Sensitive
- Gentle
- Intellectual
- Outgoing
- Playful
- Enthusiastic
- Inventive
- Efficient
- Caring
- Friendly *or*
- Strategic

So everyone gets a warm, fuzzy glow from the assessment. It's happiness all round.

So there is the 'science', questioned by other science. What good is this to you as a leader?

Avoid using MBTI to support or guide recruitment decisions. Even the owners have said that it shouldn't be abused for this purpose. Use your own intuition and use a sensible and objective process. Identify the competences that you need the recruit to demonstrate in order to be successful in the role. Look for evidence of these competences in their CV or covering letter.

Ask competency-based questions in the interview, and analyse the answers you get.

Get your team to join in the interview process so that you not only benefit from their intuition but also their expertise. This will also show them (and the applicants) that you respect and value your team members and their judgement.

If appropriate, set real pass or fail tests for people applying for the job; there are many 'ability battery' tests available that give you a genuine understanding of an applicant's reasoning skills, mathematical agility and linguistic ability.

Plan a sensible, welcoming but testing induction programme for the new starter once you have found the person you want.

Use the probation period to ensure that the skills, abilities and motivations that you were presented with in the recruitment process match up to the person who has joined the team.

So what are the big takeaways here?

- **MBTI can be helpful for teambuilding activities** but if someone wants you to use it in recruitment just say 'No'.
- **Make the effort to assess and select the long way round** rather than trying to go for a quick shortcut such as MBTI.
- **Remember that sometimes that which appears scientific, or is** widely accepted as scientific is in fact not quite all people crack it up to be.

Sources

www.vox.com/2014/7/15/5881947/myers-briggs-personality-test-meaningless

www.indiana.edu/~jobtalk/HRMWebsite/hrm/articles/develop/mbti.pdf

See also

Chapter 1 – Spreadsheets alone do not a judgement make

Chapter 12 – It takes all sorts to make a world

Chapter 33 – Find out what your followers think about you, and talk to them about it!

21 MANAGEMENT AND LEADERSHIP... A HOT TOPIC! BUT FOR WHOM?

Your management and leadership skills are important to you. But they are a heck of a lot more important to the people you manage or lead

Britain's Chartered Institute of Personnel and Development commissions regular research into relevant topics in the UK employment market.

It conducted an online survey of 2,000 UK employees in 2012; the respondents were selected and weighted to be representative of the UK workforce in relation to sector and size (private, public, voluntary), industry type and full-time/part-time working by gender.

The survey covered a wide range of topics including job satisfaction and engagement, employee attitudes towards their managers, focus on management development, pressure at work, work/life balance, employee attitudes in relation to the economic downturn and people's job-seeking situation.

This chapter concerns itself only with the section of the focus on employee attitude to their managers.

Of the total respondents some 28 per cent managed one or more people. 35 per cent of the males were managers and 21 per cent of the females.

Overall, 35 per cent of respondents who reported they managed one or more people were in the voluntary sector, followed by 30 per cent in the public sector and 27 per cent in the private sector.

On the whole, the respondents reckoned that their managers were committed to the organization (74 per cent) and that their managers treated team members fairly (71 per cent). So, generally speaking, managers aren't thought of as doing a bad job.

When you look into the detail of the survey there are some valuable nuggets to be found about people's day-to-day behaviours as managers, as perceived by the people they manage.

It is of course important to remember that managers are people/ employees and team members as well as being managers; it is not simply an 'us and them' situation.

The first interesting discovery was the relative importance that respondents placed on the required skills for success in their roles. They were asked 'How important do you consider each of the following skills as contributing to your effectiveness in your management role?' and the table below shows the percentages of respondents selecting the relevant skill as 'very important'.

People management skills	62
Operational management skills	47
Technical expertise	38
Organization/planning/project management skills	43
Managing finances/budgets	28
Monitoring of work process	36

The single most important skillset for managers regardless of their sector, is people management skills, and yet a large number of people are promoted to management responsibility on the grounds of their technical competence.

That is the 'big picture' element of the respondents' approach, but then there are some related results that are also very interesting.

There is a significant contrast between how managers say they manage people and the views of employees towards their managers.

- For example, 50 per cent of managers reported that they meet each team member every week. However, only 17 per cent of respondents said that they met with their manager weekly. In fact, people reported that their manager met them less frequently than once a month. A 'meeting' is a moveable feast so people were also asked not just about frequency of these meetings but also duration. Again there were interesting differences of opinion.
- Asked 'How much time overall per month do you spend talking to each person you manage about their workload, objectives and any other work-related issues?' 64 per cent of all managers reported spending more than 30 minutes per month per person. However, 62 per cent of people reported that their manager spent less than 30 minutes per month on this activity. Having a useful and productive meeting, and spending time in a meeting, is also a movable feast, so people were asked what was discussed in those meetings.
- The gulf between what managers reported was always discussed and what the managed thought was always discussed was again significant:

Topic discussed	Manager report %	Team member report %	Difference %
Achieving objectives	33	18	15
Instructions	23	16	7
Performance feedback	46	17	29
Praise and recognition	63	19	44
Joint problem-solving	40	15	25
Coaching	30	6	24
Personal development	20	7	13
Manager listening	80	38	42
Innovative ideas from the team member	31	15	16
Team member's 'wellbeing'	51	19	32

A certain amount of licence may be given to differences of interpretation; for instance I list a discussion as being a 'coaching' session, but the employee may have listed it as being about solving a problem or developing their abilities.

However, even given this degree of margin the differences overall are significant: managers think that they listen but the managed clearly don't feel as if they are listened to.

Not surprisingly these results correlate to the levels of satisfaction people have with their immediate manager. Managers were asked how satisfied they thought their people were with them as managers. People were asked how satisfied they actually were with their managers.

The differences between perception and reality were again quite wide:

	Manager opinion	Managed opinion	Difference
Very satisfied	15	24	9
Satisfied	65	34	31
Neither satisfied nor dissatisfied	19	26	7
Dissatisfied	1	11	10
Very dissatisfied	0	5	5

There are several interesting points that come out of this table:

First, that actually managers are very 'popular' with a larger number of their staff than they expected to be.

However, they are grossly overestimating their success in satisfying the bulk of the team the bulk of the time.

They are also making an inaccurate presumption about the proportion of their team that really don't care/are neutral

They are significantly (and possibly dangerously) underestimating the levels of active dissatisfaction with their management abilities.

OK, there are the raw scores, what can you do to make use of this to improve your leadership and management of your people?

'People management' skills are deemed to be the single most important skillset in determining and contributing to the effectiveness of a manager. So as a manager and leader you need to be dedicating a significant of your time and/or intelligent effort to managing the people in your team. Yet the survey suggests that many managers (62 per cent) are actually spending less than 30 minutes per month with each team member. Bearing in mind that, even calculating on a seven-and-a-half hour day, there are 9,000 minutes in a working month, this means that more than 60 per cent of managers spend less than 0.3 per cent of their time actually managing each staff member; the rest of their time is spent on other technical, operational and customer-related activities.

So the message here is: '**Take the time to lead and manage.**' This may require you to learn and discipline yourself to delegate more of the operational and technical duties, or you may need to simply find ways to improve your personal efficiency to free up time to manage. Doing this should also allow you the time to improve that 83 per cent of people who report that they have time with their manager less than once a month.

The two biggest gaps with regard to 'quality' of manager/ employee discussions were the lack of 'praise and recognition' and the lack of 'manager listening'. If you have a team member working for you and you are not on the brink of sacking them for incompetence then they must be doing things right/well. So the next message is: '**Catch people doing things right.**' Yes people are paid to do things right but a simple word or two of praise from you will have a major effect on people's sense of wellbeing and it costs nothing. If it helps, there is a welter of suggestion on the web of ways to do this; for example, http://www.citehr.com/ 235290-100-ways-saying-well-done-business-process.html. Some of the suggestions are a bit toe-curling but the gist is there.

Other than catching people doing things right, managers also need to listen more. This is counterintuitive in two ways:

1. Managers are often thought of as being managers (and are generally paid more) because they have the answers to the questions people ask. But... 'The wise manager doesn't give the right answers, but poses the right questions and listens to the answers'.
2. 'Listening' is seen as a passive activity; if you are listening then the control of the meeting is in the hands of the person speaking; your staff member. This is only a problem where you have to keep control due to time pressures. Refer back to the earlier message about taking time to manage; dedicate the time to listening to your people.

So what are the big takeaways here?

- **Don't assume that your people have the same opinions of your strengths and weaknesses that you have;** take time to ask them and find out what they really think.
- **Take time to manage people,** listen to them, observe them.
- **Remember that you may be doing better than you imagine!**

Source

www.cipd.co.uk/binaries/employee-outlook_2012-sprng.pdf

See also

Chapter 4 – I read it, but what the heck did it mean?

Chapter 10 – The five-step ladder to increased success

Chapter 31 – Meetings (n); Events where people get together (eventually) and waste a lot more time than they need to

Chapter 33 – Find out what your followers think about you, and talk to them about it!

Chapter 39 – Trust in your virtual team

Chapter 40 – You can NOT be serious!

22 LOOK AFTER THE VICTIMS BUT LOOK AFTER THE SURVIVORS FIRST

If you have to make redundancies, do all you can to mitigate the negative effects on the people you rely on in the future

Rifting, rightsizing, downsizing, redundancy programme, lay-offs, excess-reduction or smart-sizing, call it what you will. When an organization reduces its headcount through anything other than natural staff turnover there are two outcomes for the individual in its workforce.

You are either a leaver or a survivor.

The impact of the initiative on the leavers is self-evident; they leave. They may become unemployed, they may retire, they may change career or find another job.

The people who keep their jobs are the survivors. They are expected to continue to work diligently for the employer that gave them a second chance.

Anecdotal evidence has suggested that survivors are not always grateful for that second chance and that organizations shouldn't rely on that expected goodwill.

Cranfield School of Management (specifically Kusum Sahdev and Dr Susan Vinnicombe) produced a report in 1998 that looked into and contains a wide variety of valuable information in regard to downsizing as an activity.

The report is based upon a series of interviews and then survey responses from HR managers and directors in the UK employment market. They specify the importance of the survey group as much of the previous work in this topic has been carried out in the USA where employment law and protection of employees is (or at least was) somewhat less stringent than in the UK.

Initially, they interviewed 10 HR practitioners whose organizations had gone through downsizing within the past 12 months. From those interviews they developed the question set for the survey, which was responded to by 90 HR directors and managers out of a pool of 1,000 similar executives. Out of the 90 returned questionnaires, 60 organizations had downsized in the previous three years. The sample represented a significant cross-section of the workforce in the UK, taking into account the size of the organizations in terms of number of employees.

Staff population	Sample proportion
501–1,000	8.9%
1,001–2,500	41.1%
2,501–5,000	19.6%
5,001–10,000	7.2%
More than 10,000	23.2%

The split between private and public sectors was roughly 60/40.

Although a small majority, 55.4 per cent, of the respondents were from the south-east of the UK, the remaining 45 per cent were well spread across the rest of the nation.

Sector representation was as follows:

- 23.2 per cent manufacturing
- 16.1 per cent local government
- 12.5 per cent finance and banking
- 12.5 per cent from the health service
- 35.7 per cent covered a combination of IT, services, transportation, engineering, telecommunications and utilities.

The rationale for downsizing

The first discovery of the study was that downsizing is not always solely a symptom of a 'problem'. While about 15 per cent of respondents quoted cost reductions and cost control as reasons for the decision to downsize (and a lack of funding was also quoted by 25 per cent of organizations), other reasons to reduce headcount include:

- restructuring
- relayering
- changing organizational culture
- technological advancement
- strategic outsourcing
- multi-skilling
- adapting to new competencies.

The alternatives

In terms of strategies to avoid downsizing, 48.2 per cent didn't use alternatives but relied solely on cutting the headcount.

More than one method was used by some organizations.

37.5 per cent used contracting out and redeployments of certain staff and categories of staff.

Part-time opportunities were used by only 16.1 per cent.

Reduced hours contracts were only offered by 10.7 per cent of the organizations.

Other methods used included:

- recruitment moratoria
- nonrenewal of fixed-term contracts
- termination of temporary contracts
- overtime bans.

It appears that on the whole, employers preferred one-off reductions in size rather than being more flexible and offering interim solutions.

Support to the leavers

Generally, organizations were 'humane' to the people leaving:

78.9 per cent provided counselling and support via their own HR team

50.9 per cent used the leaver's own line managers to provide support (talk about being fed by the hand that bit you!)

And 68.4 per cent paid external career counsellors/outplacement consultants

(There was obviously some overlap with some organizations providing two or more sources of support)

Support to the survivors

Sadly, the support given to survivors is generally lacking:

- on average, about 5 per cent of the workforce received some training for their new roles (where they were 'picking up the slack' resulting from their colleagues' departure)
- about 20 per cent of the population got some sort of counselling on a group or 1:1 basis.

There is little evidence of any attempt to rebuild the changed dynamic of the work teams.

Survivor reactions

Respondents defined survivor reactions as:

'fearful' 'defensive about their roles' 'task-focused' 'suffering a sense of loss of colleagues'	'most' or 'some' survivors
'let down by the company' 'angry' 'bitter' 'trapped'	'some' or 'a few'

It is worth remembering here that 'survivors' refers to all the remaining staff and management of the organization... so the atmosphere and culture of the organizations was summed up by the words in the left hand column... not a nice place to be 40 hours a week!

This was evidenced by the fact that:

- Stress levels were reported to be up in 75 per cent of cases
- An individual's commitment to achieving targets dropped in some 19 per cent of cases
- Loyalty to the organization dropped in 47 per cent of cases
- Motivation decreased in 45 per cent of cases
- Trust in the organization and its management fell in 66 per cent of cases
- And more than 70 per cent of people were reported to feel that the fun had gone out of their workplace.

The 'bottom line'

Overall performance revealed interesting outcomes:

- 49.1 per cent of HR directors/managers felt that performance had actually gone up
- 45.6 per cent felt that downsizing did not make any difference to performance levels and 5.3 per cent felt that it had gone down.

However, staff turnover increased in some 30 per cent of cases; many of the people who were kept on in the redundancy programme quit shortly afterwards, which brings with it significant potential costs of recruitment and induction. With stress levels rocketing and commitment motivation and loyalty all down, it has to be asked whether this improvement in performance is likely to be sustainable.

The report goes on to look specifically at the future opportunities and challenges for the HR community – so as this book isn't aimed at (exclusively) HR people, we will not dwell further on the study, but look at what it means for leaders and managers.

1. If faced with the possibility of making redundancies in reaction to any market conditions, look first at the alternative options. Many in the modern workforce would welcome the

opportunity for part-time work, casual work, a contractor arrangement or a subcontract. Perhaps they wouldn't ask for one but as an alternative to losing their livelihood entirely in one fell swoop it would probably be a nicer option for the individual and have a less severe effect on the survivors.

2. If you do go down the downsizing route, don't forget the survivors: surviving managers will need the resources to rebuild their teams, they'll need time to manage, coach and support them through this transition. They may need extra management training and development to improve/widen their management skills. Operational staff will need technical development to help them pick up the slack more effectively; this isn't just about milking more out of the remaining bodies but helping them to reduce their stress and long-hours alternative. It also demonstrates a commitment to them and their career; this reduces the fear of being on the next tranche of bloodletting – no one invests in a person just before axing them.

3. Keep the 'fun' things – be it the Christmas party or the social club, inject some fun activities into the teambuilding resources. Give people and their immediate supervisors the encouragement and resources to inject a bit of light-heartedness back into the workplace.

4. Make as solid a commitment to people as you can to the fact that the redundancies are now at an end. If you aren't high enough up the organization to do this on your own initiative, chase your boss and your boss's boss to get the green light to do so. The sooner you can do this the sooner the survivors start to feel like the lucky ones. The more you can do this the faster people will regain some trust in the management that they perceive has let them down.

Anecdotal evidence from the author's own experience is that as the leavers resettle they tend to keep in touch with their former colleagues... the colleagues then look at the leavers' new sense of purpose, compare it to their own feelings: 'fearful', 'defensive about their roles', 'let down by the company', 'angry', 'bitter' and 'trapped'...

So what are the big takeaways here?

* Spread the word that the survivors are critical to future success, so just keeping their jobs is rarely enough.
* If you have had to let people go, get out to the survivors and rebuild your team.
* Remember that even though 'jobs for life' are a thing of the past, people still like to belong.

Source

https://dspace.lib.cranfield.ac.uk/retrieve/483/coareport910

See also

Chapter 5 – 'Workers' play time' – is it really worth it?

Chapter 7 – 'An employee's workspace is his castle... or should be!'

Chapter 9 – Rule No. 1: Never volunteer for anything. NOT!

Chapter 26 – Learning; it's a generational thing

Chapter 28 – What happens when you (or someone you manage) make decisions under pressure?

Chapter 35 – 'Trust me, I'm a manager'

Chapter 39 – Trust in your virtual team

23 WE'RE WORKING NINE TO FIVE – IT'S NO WAY TO MAKE A LIVING

Part time doesn't mean second class... it just means part time

For many people the perception is simple; if you have a 'job' you work nine to five, five days a week. You have Saturday and Sunday off and that is it. This is a perception that is perhaps a lot less true than many people think. In 2009 the Australian Bureau of Statistics collated data from several contemporary governmental censuses and published a report entitled 'Patterns in Work'. The report provides data relating to people's working patterns and preferences and given that Australia is a developed nation with an ethnically diverse population of more than 20 million and a wide industrial/commercial base there is no reason to believe that the working patterns in the country are significantly different from any other developed nation.

According to the report, some 30 per cent of the working population was working part time, working fewer than 35 hours a week (in all their jobs combined). This proportion had increased from 16 per cent 30 years previously.

Some 20 per cent of the working population worked on a casual basis, regardless of the hours they worked they had no formal contract and were not entitled to paid holiday or sick leave. (Note that this doesn't include 'owner/managers of incorporated enterprises' (OMIEs). These are people who work in their own limited liability company, such as contractors.)

17 per cent of the people in work were owner/managers; they worked a full week and took their own responsibility for holiday or sickness cover. This group included all forms of owner/

manager, whether they were a limited liability company or not and regardless of whether they employed others or not. The proportion of owner/managers had fluctuated between 20 per cent and 17 per cent over the previous decade.

63 per cent of the working population was categorized as 'employed'; they worked more than 35 hours a week and were entitled by law to paid holiday and/or paid sick leave. Over the previous decade this number had fluctuated between 59 per cent and 63 per cent.

The report then gives some of the characteristics of the people in the different employment categories:

Selected characteristics	Units	Casual	Other	Total	Owner/ manager	Total employed
Average age	years	33.7	39.2	37.9	46.4	39.5
Proportion who are women	%	55.8	45.5	48.0	32.3	45.1
Proportion who work part-time	%	70.0	16.7	29.5	28.2	29.3
Average hours usually worked by part-timers	no.	16.3	23.1	19.2	18.9	19.2
Average hours usually worked by full-timers	no.	42.7	42.9	42.8	51.4	44.4
Number	'000	2,075.7	6,586.6	8,662.2	1,972.2	10,634.5

The ABS Survey of Employment Arrangements, Retirement and Superannuation, which was conducted in 2007, asked people to describe some of their usual work patterns and then asked them what patterns they would prefer to work (taking into account the effect this might have on their income).

64 per cent of those employed people surveyed usually worked all of their hours during daylight hours, defined as between seven in the morning and seven in the evening.

Almost all of these people (96 per cent), who only worked during daytime hours liked it that way.

Among the remaining 36 per cent of employed people who usually worked some or all of their hours at night, over two-thirds (68 per cent) actually preferred to be working some or all of their hours at night.

Similarly, among the 63 per cent of employed people who didn't usually work at all on the weekend, virtually all (96 per cent) preferred to have their weekend off.

Of the other 37 per cent of employed people who did usually work on the weekend, almost two-thirds (65 per cent) were following their preference for working some or all of their hours on the weekend.

People who *usually* worked over the weekend and preferred to work over the weekend were a diverse group. For example:

- 30 per cent of people were casual employees
- 26 per cent were owner/managers
- 59 per cent were male
- 26 per cent were aged 15–24 years
- 17 per cent were aged 55 years or older.

This is in comparison to *all* employed people where the figures are:

- 20 per cent were casual employees
- 20 per cent were owner/managers
- 55 per cent were male
- 17 per cent were aged 15–24 years
- 15 per cent were aged 55 years or older.

65 per cent of employed people felt they were working close to their preferred number of hours.

14 per cent of people wanted to work more hours than they were usually working

21 per cent would have preferred to work fewer hours for less money.

Part-timers who were *dissatisfied* with the number of hours they were working tended to want more hours, whereas full-time employees who were dissatisfied tended to want fewer hours.

People who only just worked full-time hours (i.e. those who usually worked between 35 and 39 hours a week) were among the most content: only 13 per cent wanted to spend more time working.

Of the people who usually worked a longer than 49-hour week, 51 per cent were happy with the number of hours they worked.

Only 3 per cent of this group actually wanted more hours, while 46 per cent would have preferred to work fewer hours and accept a commensurate drop in pay (where appropriate, i.e. where the employees are paid overtime).

24 per cent of employed people who wanted to work fewer hours felt that their work and family responsibilities were 'rarely, if ever', in balance.

At the same time, 41 per cent of them felt that their work and family responsibilities were 'often if not always' in balance.

Qualitative responses in this area were that some people wanted to work less mainly to be able to spend more time caring for children, but the single most commonly cited main reason for wanting to work fewer hours was to spend more time on social and/or recreational activities.

There is the data, what use is it to you as a leader?

1. Many organizations offer flexible working practices and though they are often formally available to all, there is frequently a perception that they are available for family employees. Single or childless employees need not apply as they will be judged unfavourably. But the survey showed that

'the single most commonly cited main reason for wanting to work fewer hours was to spend more time on social and/or recreational activities'. So make sure that the letter and the spirit of the policy is available to all, spending less time at work isn't a statement of lower loyalty or commitment, it is a demonstration of a balanced individual and a more sustainable employment situation. It is better to keep a good employee for fewer hours a week than to lose them altogether.

2. When reorganizing or looking to make the sort of changes that often result in downsizing, remember that, of the full time employees, 46 per cent may prefer to work fewer hours and accept a commensurate drop in pay. So before embarking on a headcount-cutting project, ask the current workforce if they would like to accommodate the organizational needs without the mass disruption of downsizing.

3. Listen to the voice of the workforce, look at the number of people still working 'out of hours': if people are working long hours, remember that '46 per cent may prefer to work fewer hours'. That means that nearly half of your staff may be unhappy about the long hours they are having to work. And that '24 per cent of employed people who wanted to work fewer hours felt that their work and family responsibilities were "rarely, if ever," in balance.' People's families are a major influence and an influence that is increasing. When long hours become the norm, many people will vote with their feet and depart the organization leaving you with significant bills to recruit and induct new people. Give serious consideration to recruiting someone on a part-time and/or casual basis to take up the extra workload even if you can't justify another full-time employee.

So what are the big takeaways here?

- Ask people how they prefer to work rather than imposing an all or nothing approach to a job or no job.
- Be flexible about other people's working patterns; we all understand that occasionally we have to make sacrifices, but not on a permanent or very frequent basis.
- Remember that in the 21st century there are often options for employees; they are less beholden to their employer for their livelihood.

Source

www.abs.gov.au/AUSSTATS/abs@.nsf/Lookup/4102.0Main+Feat
ures50Dec+2009

See also

Chapter 12 – It takes all sorts to make a world

Chapter 13 – To be (here) or not to be (here), that is the question

Chapter 24 – You don't have to love the quitters but at least
listen to them

Chapter 32 – ROWE, ROWE, ROWE your boat!

Chapter 39 – Trust in your virtual team

24 YOU DON'T HAVE TO LOVE THE QUITTERS BUT AT LEAST LISTEN TO THEM

*Someone leaving your employment may be seen as disloyal...
but that may mean that you haven't earned their loyalty!*

The Chartered Institute of Personnel and Development calculates the average cost of recruiting an employee in the UK at between £8,200 and £12,000. So once you have recruited a decent employee, at any level in the hierarchy, it makes financial sense to try to keep hold of them. Notwithstanding that it is widely recognized that some turnover is a positive thing, it is also a clear truism that too many people leaving is financially costly and has potentially detrimental effects on customer service, internal relationships and operational continuity.

This chapter looks at two studies that have been done looking at why people quit their employer; one in the UK and one in Bangladesh. The two have been chosen since one relates staff retention in a mature, developed economy with relatively high levels of protective employment legislation and the other relates to an emerging economy engaged in rapid economic growth and relatively low employment protection law. It is unlikely that it costs between 942,000 and 1.4 million Bangladeshi Taka to recruit one person.

The UK

Benchmark Recruit, a Sheffield-based recruitment consultancy, surveyed more than 3,000 individuals to assess their declared justification for quitting their previous role. The results are tabulated below, ranked in order of magnitude.

Primary reason for leaving	%
1 Lack of faith in the leadership team	22.58
2 = Feeling unappreciated	19.35
2 = Feeling disengaged/demotivated	19.35
3 Lack of financial reward	12.90
4 Redundancy	9.68
5 No belief in the company's service/product	6.45
6 = Travel/location	3.23
6 = Clash with colleague	3.23
6 = Poor relationship with line manager	3.23

It is interesting to see the apparent similarity between the #1 reason and the last one in the list; people cited a lack of faith in the leadership of the organization as the single biggest reason to quit, whereas a 'poor relationship with their line manager' was actually pretty insignificant. This tells us that the relationship can be pretty good even though there is no faith. In other words: 'I quite like you; you're a nice person, but I have little respect for your abilities.'

Second equal is a pair of responses that ring bells with so many of the other studies in this book. Feeling unappreciated and feeling disengaged or demotivated. Each of these accounts for 20 per cent of the people who quit.

So more than 60 per cent of an organization's drain is down to three causes and those three causes all relate to the behaviours of management. If management was more open about its decision-making process and more consistent in its communication and listening with the shop floor, then people would feel more engaged and have greater faith (obviously succeeding in the market would help enormously as well!).

The survey also asked people to 'describe' their current role by putting it into one of four categories:

1. My perfect job (25.5 per cent)
2. A stepping stone in my career (38.5 per cent)

3. A stop gap to pay the mortgage (16.5 per cent)

4. A dead end job (19.5 per cent)

While this looks potentially frightening it is worth a little analysis.

A quarter of people are in their perfect job; so long as they can be engaged and appreciated they will stay and will apply discretionary effort.

Nearly 40 per cent are in a stepping stone period; good – this means that they are thinking about their career and this role is *right for them at the moment*. Nurture and develop these people and they are your management/tech specialists of the future. Treat them well and even if they leave for something better (as opposed to leaving you in desperation), they may serve well as alumni in the future or even return to your fold with greater expertise.

One in six of your people may be there simply to pay the mortgage. Although they may hit your bottom line with replacement costs at some stage in the future, so long as they are managed well, they will still give you a fair day's work for a fair day's pay in the interim.

One in four sees this as a dead-end job. As with the previous category, they may leave shortly. Your challenge is to make sure that though they may not be going anywhere, they remain happy and productive in the time they are with you.

Bangladesh

Three academics from the Bangladesh University of Business and Technology and Port City International University (Md. Jahangir Alam, Md. Mahofuzur Rahman and Md. Farid Hossain Talukder) (*see* Sources, below) carried out this study and surveyed 103 employees from different organizations who had left their previous jobs or had declared an intention to leave. The areas of sampling were mainly Dhaka and Chittagong: Bangladesh's two largest cities.

The demographic of the study group was as follows:

Male	86.67 per cent
Female	13.33 per cent
Public Sector	3.8 per cent
Private Sector	6.2 per cent

Their questionnaire used a 1 to 5 scale, so people were rating a series of factors that contributed to their decision to quit.

The results, in order of influence, were:

1. Low salary
2. Absence of pension
3. Inappropriate performance appraisal and recognition
4. Less scope for personal growth and development
5. Low incremental increase in income
6. Lack of bonus
7. Inadequate number of paid hours
8. Inadequate facilities (accommodation, transport, etc.)
9. Excessive pressure
10. Low job satisfaction
11. Poor management

Clearly there are some differences between employee attitudes and expectations in an emerging economy and in a developed economy. In Bangladesh the money issue, a typical Maslow 'hygiene factor', is top of the list, whereas the British survey surprised the survey team when they saw that money was less important than several other criteria.

To put the outcomes of both surveys together they look like this:

Bangladesh	UK
1 Low salary	1 Lack of faith in the leadership team
2 Absence of pension	2 = Feeling unappreciated
3 Inappropriate performance appraisal and recognition	2 = Feeling disengaged/demotivated
4 Less scope for personal growth	3 Lack of financial reward

5 Low incremental increase in income	4 Redundancy
6 Lack of bonus	5 No belief in the company's service/product
7 Inadequate number of paid hours	6 = Travel/location
8 Inadequate facilities (accommodation, transport, etc.)	6 = Clash with colleague
9 Excessive pressure	6 = Poor relationship with line manager
10 Low job satisfaction	
11 Poor management	

However, if we look a bit closer at the Bangladeshi results we see that the survey separated 'salary' from 'incremental increase in income', 'bonus' and the 'number of paid hours'. These factors came in at numbers 5, 6 & 7, after 'inappropriate performance appraisal and recognition' and 'scope for personal growth and development'.

The results, though clearly not the same, are actually much more similar than they at first appear. The overwhelming message is that human beings are remarkably similar but that if you are managing a global organization be aware that there are differences in different parts of the world.

So what are the big takeaways here?

- **Ask around your own workplace;** what made people leave their previous jobs?
- **Look at the lists of reasons people quit;** then look at your management style and your organization… what might your present colleagues be saying in a couple of years' time when they are asked why they left you?
- **Remember that there is no silver bullet to keeping good people;** it is a package of criteria ranging from the day-to-day thank yous to the annual salary review.

Sources

www.cipd.co.uk/NR/rdonlyres/C725AF28-202C-41FC-99CD-0EABB5A5B28D/0/4357MBAbookletWEB.pdf

www.cipd.co.uk/NR/rdonlyres/746F1183-3941-4E6A-9EF6-135C29AE22C9/0/recruitmentsurv07.pdf

https://www.academia.edu/8403929/Identifying_the_Reasons_for_which_People_Quit_their_Jobs_An_Empirical_Study_in_the_Organizations_of_Bangladesh

See also

Chapter 5 – 'Workers' play time' – is it really worth it?

Chapter 18 – Leadership and leaders; let's get complex

Chapter 21 – Management and leadership... a hot topic! But for whom?

Chapter 23 – We're working nine to five – it's no way to make a living

Chapter 26 – Learning; it's a generational thing

Chapter 32 – ROWE, ROWE, ROWE your boat!

Chapter 34 – Talent management – have you got your EVP right?

25 IS TEAMWORK ALWAYS THE ANSWER?

If your teamworking ethic is too good it can become dangerous; you need to have some disagreement and conflict

You are the boss. You have a team. The team is high-functioning; there is a strong degree of cohesiveness, a commitment to achieve the goals and a strong sense of urgency. Your people think alike. There is seldom conflict in the team. You don't spend a lot of time talking round and round the issues. The focus is on rapid decision-making, agility and action. You personally don't necessarily make all the decisions, they are consensus decisions; the team all agrees and then all support the decisions. You run a high-performing team.

But...

The decision in the early 1960s to launch the ill-fated Bay of Pigs invasion was taken by a group operating just like yours.

The decision to go ahead with the 1986 *Challenger* space mission (the ill-fated rocket exploding shortly after take-off killing all seven astronauts) was taken by a group operating like yours.

The decision to launch Gulf War II and the invasion of Afghanistan...

Those teams were operating in what is now called 'groupthink'.

Is your team in danger of falling into a similar trap?

Irving Janis coined the term 'groupthink', in his 1982 work, *Groupthink: Psychological studies of policy decisions and fiascoes* (Houghton Mifflin).

Groupthink tends to occur in highly cohesive groups in which the group members' desire for consensus, cohesion and action becomes more important than objective evaluation of problems and potential outcomes. When this happens the result can be a serious deterioration in mental efficiency, poor analytical thought and lax moral judgement, while all the time the appearance is of efficiency, teamwork and effectiveness.

Groupthink is most likely to emerge when:

- the group is very cohesive
- the group becomes insulated from qualified outsiders, and/or
- the leader promotes his or her own favoured solution.

Fred Lunenburg, of Sam Houston State University in Texas, has carried out a study of the literature and assessments of a wide range of academics on the subject. He has produced a very comprehensive document, outlining Janis's identified symptoms of groupthink. This helps leaders spot the difference between healthy consensus and cohesion and the dangerous slide into groupthink.

He also outlines Janis's strategies to avoid groupthink and obviously the unintended consequences of it.

Symptoms that suggest your team may be moving into dangerous areas:

1. **Illusions of invulnerability** – A majority or all of the team members develop an illusion of invulnerability; this is often the result of a string of successes and achievements. Longstanding high-performing teams are hence very vulnerable. Unfortunately, this causes them to start to take extreme risks based on optimistic assumptions. There is a belief that 'we've done it before therefore we will, of course, do it again'.
2. **Irrational rationalization** – Team members collectively and individually rationalize in order to discount or minimize any warnings, caveats or concerns. They may rationalize away concerns about the likelihood of problems or the impact of those problems. In short, they 'extenuate the negative'.

3. **An overwhelming sense of 'right'** – The team develops an unquestioned belief in the group's moral superiority; as a result it ignores/waives normal ethical or moral consequences of the decisions. It may be verbalized as: 'for the greater good'.

4. **Stereotyping non-members** – Group members develop stereotyped views of outsiders in opposition as being either:

   * too evil and/or
   * too weak and/or
   * too stupid and/or
   * too insignificant...
   * ...to be considered, negotiated with, or respected.

5. **Internal policing of the 'team' ethos** – Team members turn on any member who expresses strong doubts about, or argues against, any of the team's attitudes, illusions or commitments. They declare almost any dissent as disloyalty or demonstrating a lack of commitment to the other members of the team or the team's objectives/ethos. 'If you aren't with us, you are against us.'

6. **Self-criticism** – Individuals censure themselves for any deviations from the team's consensus, minimizing the importance of their individual doubts and counterarguments relative to the team's cohesion. 'I had a tiny niggling doubt, it was nothing really, I was just being paranoid, but now I see that I was wrong.'

7. **The illusion of unanimity** – There is an illusion of shared unanimity concerning judgements conforming to the majority view. This is partly due to #6 above and is strengthened by the assumption that the resulting absence of dissent is equal to consent. 'So we are all agreed then, good, next item.'

8. **The appearance of 'Mindguards'** – Some team members appoint themselves as guard dogs and gatekeepers, 'protecting' the group from external information or opinions that might question their shared comfort about their outputs.

How you can avoid groupthink.

1. Actively encourage the airing of objections and doubt, where necessary appointing someone (possibly on a rolling basis) to act as 'Devil's Advocate'.

2. When delegating, or when initiating decision-making and/or policy-making to a team, avoid stating your own preferences and expectations.
3. Split your team into two sub-teams to work on the same question, each carrying out its deliberations separately. Clearly this appears to be unproductive and potentially competitive, but it can have major benefits if it avoids groupthink.
4. When considering alternatives, again split the team into sub-teams to consider them independently, then get the sub-teams back together to compare recommendations.
5. Encourage each member of the team to periodically discuss the team's deliberations with trusted associates and report their discussions back to the group.
6. Invite outside experts, or qualified colleagues within the organization, but from outside your team, to your team meetings. Encourage them to challenge the views of the team and its members.
7. Show respect for rivals and other stakeholders, actively seek out and take seriously any warning signals from these parties. Take time to consider these parties' reactions to your decision.
8. After reaching a consensus about what seems to be the best course of action, hold a dedicated meeting at which you and the other team members are expected to express as vividly as you can what could go wrong for the team and its chosen solution.

Groupthink is a very dangerous phenomenon for a leader. It often sneaks up on you after a long period of success when it seems that everything your team touches turns to gold. It often exhibits signs similar to a high-performing team – a cohesive group that seldom disagrees, appears to be efficient and is action oriented. However, groupthink bites and the fallout is considerable. Usually when it bites, it is the leader who gets the blame as people start claiming that the culture was one where dissent was discouraged and yes-men (or yes-women) thrived.

So what are the big takeaways here?

- **Ask people to challenge the status quo and the consensus.** Phrase your questions carefully, ask: 'What could go wrong?' 'How could this go wrong?' 'How could this be perceived?' rather than asking if people agree with the team decision (or your decision).
- **Appoint a Devil's Advocate to challenge decisions.** Then be seen to treat that person's challenges seriously.
- **Remember that groupthink can look like a high-performing team,** so if your team is currently performing well, don't rest on your laurels. Beware groupthink!

Source

www.nationalforum.com/Electronic%20Journal%20Volumes/
Lunenburg,%20Fred%20C.%20Group%20Decision%20
Making%20IJMBA%20V13%20N1%202010.pdf

See also

Chapter 12 – It takes all sorts to make a world

Chapter 18 – Leadership and leaders; let's get complex

Chapter 21 – Management and leadership... a hot topic! But for whom?

Chapter 28 – What happens when you (or someone you manage) make decisions under pressure?

26 LEARNING; IT'S A GENERATIONAL THING

Don't believe everything you hear about the 'youth of today',
but do believe this: it is based on science

When reading the newspapers or listening to the news one often hears references to the exasperation shown by employers at the problems of the younger generation. They have problems with basic mathematics, their written work is of a poor standard, they have short attention spans and unrealistically high expectations of their career.

How realistic is this media image of this entire generation?

If it is realistic, what can you do about it as a manager and leader?

Research by Carina Paine Schofield and Sue Honoré (both of Ashridge Business School in the UK) has identified the 'missing skills' of the younger generation. They also assessed and developed recommendations for those concerned with this generation's development. Finally, they outline the potentially positive impact of this group on the future of learning for all generations.

Their study was more holistic than looking solely at the younger generation; they included people up to the age of 63 to ensure that their results actually compared generations rather than making assumptions about previous age ranges while studying the younger group.

They defined the generational categories by birth year as:

- Baby Boomers – 1946–1963
- Early Generation X – 1964–1976
- Late Generation X – 1977–1981
- Generation Y – 1982–2002

The younger generation they were focusing on is the 'Generation Y' group, also commonly referred to as:

- millennials
- the iPod generation
- the 'me firsts'
- the Internet generation
- the echo boomers
- the Nintendo generation
- the digital generation
- generation 'why?'
- generation next
- the 'I' generation, and
- the net generation.

The study involved a detailed review of existing published material on the subject by academics and business leaders, followed by qualitative and quantitative data collection.

- 133 individuals, representing 59 organizations, from both public and private sectors undertook a series of face-to-face interviews and/or focus groups
- 692 individuals responded to an online survey (the online participants and literature review was global; the other research was UK centric)
- 284 participants completed a Kolb Learning Style Inventory.

Respondents were aged from 16 to over 63 years, representing the full range of employment-age people.

The table below summarizes the findings relevant to Generation Y respondents:

Strengths common to *all* members of Generation Y	Questioning established processes Approachability and friendliness to all ages Work/life balancing Networking outside organization Trust Lack of prejudice Flexibility Energy
Abilities which *vary* between Generation Y members	Loyalty Respect Focus/concentration/attention span IT skills Communication skills Motivation Creativity Communication skills Global outlook Teamwork Managing others Expectation of quality
Weaknesses common to *all* members of Generation Y	Budgeting/financial management Self-awareness/emotional intelligence Risk assessment/risk-taking Taking criticism Written English Analysis/deeper thinking Self-management

Outcomes

1. One outcome of the study that challenges the common perception of Generation Y, the iPod/Nintendo/Internet generation is that in spite of being very au fait with technology, the generation is not universally at home with modern *productive* technology... many struggle with common workplace applications.

2. Generation Y is also infamous for eschewing the value of memorizing information for the sake of quick recall, preferring to 'Google-it' (or any of the myriad other online information sources) at the time of need. Unfortunately, there seems to be a very significant lack of ability to analyse, judge or risk-assess that information to ensure that it makes sense or is accurate.

3. This lack of judgement and analytical skills also creates common difficulties with problem solving; where a solution is clearly right or wrong there is little issue, but where a solution is in shades of grey, many 'Generation Yers' really struggle. Their mindset (gained from the games they play(ed) and the education system they enjoyed) is to use trial and error until they succeed. They see each 'failure' as a learning opportunity in comparison to the older generations who see a failure as a failure and therefore prefer to analyse, judge, plan and then carry out a more considered course of action.

4. Although they may be great *social networkers*, many young people struggle with face-to-face communication, particularly when handling difficult messages from and to other people. This is not generally to say that they can't give feedback, but that they often lack the emotional intelligence to do so diplomatically or sensitively. Generally speaking, their self-awareness and ability to accept criticism and feedback is not brilliant.

5. Very few 'Generation Yers' have developed an innate sense of risk assessment, whether that concerns basic health and safety, or the consideration of implications and consequences of courses of action. They therefore have a tendency either to be fully risk averse or verging on reckless!

6. Many 'Generation Yers' have short attention spans and low boredom thresholds; they are more attuned to short sharp bursts of any particular activity, than to long plods.

7. #6 also manifests itself in a degree of impatience; 'Generation Yers' don't like hanging around waiting for things.

OK, there is the data from the surveys. The report's authors also go on to make recommendations regarding the development of Generation Y. Many of them spill over to the development of all other staff or offer other mutual benefit.

These are broken down into five areas:

- **High-quality learning and development in remedial business skills:** the content needs to up-skill the individuals in verbal reasoning, maths, budgeting, written English, team skills and relationship management. The style of this learning and development should be experiential, reflective and relevant to the role, not didactic or theoretical. Ideally using a blend of activities and styles.

- **Redefine career paths by the use of projects and secondments:** most learning is now informal rather than formal, and much of that is achieved on the job. Traditional career ladders do not suit modern business practice and flat hierarchies. They are also an issue with impatient Generation Y. Focus on finding ways of developing the individual, enriching learning and retaining all your good staff as well as Generation Y. Involvement in small projects alongside the main job, and secondments to other areas of the business are excellent ways to broaden your development and learning approach.

- **Provide personal one-to-one support by coaching and mentoring:** Generation Y expects more support in their growth and development than previous generations. One-to-one coaching and mentoring are seen as successful methods of retaining them and motivating them to achieve higher goals. Be aware that they are used to almost exclusively positive feedback and encouragement, so coach/mentor needs to be skilled in introducing more critical feedback, which clearly should be developmental.

- **Deliberately engineered mixed generational projects and reverse mentoring:** 'Mixed generational projects': avoid creating a project team made up of specialists in the field with similar levels of expertise, but deliberately putting a range of seniority/experience in the team. This provides learning for all team members and has been shown to break down stereotypical beliefs about different generations. It can also help avoid 'groupthink' (see Chapter 25). 'Reverse mentoring': where a more experienced employee and a Generation Y employee coach each other in different aspects (for example, office politics and use of new technology). This encourages the development of both parties and helps to drive inclusion and the sharing of ideas. The pairs need to share the same desire to make the relationship succeed.

- **Encourage value-add networking:** Generation Y has grown up in a culture where knowledge and advice can be obtained, virtually, from anywhere. These wider networks are also beginning to be exploited in the same way by older generations as well. Consider developing a network that includes your own employees and ex-employees, knowing that their contribution may continue to be high. (See Chapter 27.)

> Value-add networking is not the same as encouraging vacuous social networking, OMG, LOL ;-). But be aware that the same policies, firewalls and security processes designed to stop this activity may detrimentally affect people's ability to access value-added networking.

So what are the big takeaways here?

- **If you hear someone moaning about the youth of today**, point out two things: first, that there are inherent and valuable strengths in their differing culture and approach; second, not all Generation Y people are alike, some of them are focused, respectful, motivated and articulate.
- **If you are responsible for L&D** (and every line manager/leader IS; see Chapter 6), take into account that the general learning style of Generation Y is different from the traditional format. Exploit that for maximum impact.
- **Remember that everyone is an individual** and you need to know the individuals rather than relying on stereotypes!

Source

http://staff.ashridge.org.uk/Website/Content.nsf/FileLibrary/B89 ECF594F4B61FC802576880055F97A/$file/360_Winter09_web. pdf#page=27

See also

Chapter 30 – Managing the millennials… some new challenges

Chapter 36 – Stop paying attention to the PowerPoint® default settings!

Chapter 40 – You can NOT be serious!

27 A 'TRAINING COURSE' IS NOT THE SILVER BULLET FOR GETTING PEOPLE TO LEARN (IN FACT IT IS BARELY A BLANK CARTRIDGE)

People learn every day; you can save a lot of money and learn a lot more even if you don't go to business school

Historically, organizations used to always work on the principle that people learned by going on a training course. Many people, once they had passed their initial exams or apprenticeship, never attended another class in their entire working lives. More enlightened employers provided training for people as they rose up the ranks within their employer. Hence, training departments were formed to support this.

In the 1960s Professor Allen Tough started to research and to question this paradigm and his studies identified that, in actual fact, about 70 per cent of all 'learning projects' were initiated and planned by the learner, not the employer. His work became the foundation for many other studies into the field of adult learning, not least of which was one carried out by the Centre for Creative Leadership and published in 1996 in the book *The Career Architect Development Planner* by Michael M. Lombardo and Robert W. Eichinger. This was the book that coined the phrase '70:20:10'.

70:20:10 describes their findings relating to the sources of learning among most adults with managerial responsibilities:

- 70 per cent is learned from the hands-on experience of doing tough jobs; not just learning by mistakes but also successes.

The pertinent fact is that the learning comes from doing, rather than formal instruction or discussion.

- 20 per cent is learned from talking to and observing other people (mostly, but by no means exclusively, their boss)
- 10 per cent is learned from attending formal training/academic courses and from reading.

Not unlike the work by Mehrabian mentioned in Chapter 3, you may not like the concept of apparently fixed percentages, and the authors have been at pains to point out that 70:20:10 is not a rule but a guiding principle.

This chapter looks at a related and contemporary study published as 'The Teaching Firm: Where Productive Work and Learning Converge' from the Education Development Center Inc. of Massachusetts, USA.

This study researched more than a thousand participants in seven different organizations. It engaged in shadowing-observation and interview, in-depth individual interviews and focus groups of small teams of employees. The whole population was then subjected to a survey questionnaire which was statistically analysed. This analysis includes all aspects of the demographics of the respondents with regard to their age ethnicity, tenure, education and income. Researchers also gathered organizational data regarding goal-setting, business metrics and organizational procedures.

The authors go to some lengths to point out that their findings predicate a very high impact of the target organizations' context on the outcomes and methods. In other words, their report does not tell readers how to successfully implement informal on-the-job learning in their own organizations; this does not detract from the value of the study in a generic sense.

The report identifies and concentrates on two aspects of informal learning in a high-performing organization:

Why informal learning occurs

The report identified that individuals *seek* informal learning for personal desires with regard to their achievement.

Individuals seek to attain:

- a sense of belonging to a social group or community
- recognition from their superiors, peers and subordinates
- comfort and security from working in a safe and attractive working environment
- satisfaction from having control over their own work and output
- pride in their accomplishments and their increasing mastery of their chosen career
- satisfaction of overcoming challenges and solving problems
- pride in the sense of contributing to a larger worthwhile enterprise.

It was found that most informal learning is driven by the need to achieve these goals and this is most dramatically seen where *individual* workforce members' goals clearly link to, align with and support organizational goals.

This may seem obvious and simplistic, but since informal learning is driven by the individual not the organization, then it must be accepted that the senior management must create a culture where informal learning will occur, rather than setting informal learning as a goal in itself. In a culture where organizational goals are seen as important, the individual workforce member is fully aware of the *organizational* goals, and if he or she has personal targets that clearly relate to these goals informal learning will be more likely to happen by default.

Individual goals and targets need to be set within a culture that reduces the separation between management and employee responsibility; in other words where everyone is more empowered and less supervised. This in turn requires a situation where employees are encouraged to a take a greater part in:

- decision-making
- cost reduction
- quality and productivity improvement
- problem-solving.

And to achieve this, all employees need to understand:

- the metrics the organization uses for measuring quality and productivity
- where their role fits in the overall organization and its processes
- how to communicate effectively with their customers, be they internal or external
- how to document their processes and results

And be held accountable for their personal output.

Clearly all this requires more management and leadership than simply giving someone a job description and leaving them to get on with 'business as usual' for the next ten years.

How informal learning occurs

The report identified 13 work activities where people learned the most. By engaging in these activities people either gained knowledge or developed skills that improved their productivity. The 13 are listed below by value rather than frequency; for instance whilst peer-to-peer communication happened almost every day it produced less valuable learning per interaction than the rarer interaction with customers.

- Teaming
- Meetings
- Interacting with customers
- Supervision
- Mentoring
- Shift change
- Peer-to-peer communication
- Cross training
- Exploration
- On-the-job training

- Documentation
- Execution of one's job
- Site visits

The report gives a huge wealth of detail (the report is 297 pages long) about each of these activities, far more than can be covered here. This is a very potted summary of the best practice contained in the report.

A. **Teaming** – this is the title given to the creation of a team to address a particular problem or goal. Teams can be created from the actual work team, a cross-functional/hierarchical team or a team with specialists. People learned most when the team had:

- authority over the outcome
- resources to achieve the outcome/goal expected
- diversity of perspective
- team decision-making
- appropriate time schedules.

B. **Meetings** – informal learning occurs mainly through observation, participation and questioning. So meetings should have:

- active participation from all attendees
- clearly stated goals and agendas
- an open-minded chair who encourages open exchange of ideas and opinions.

C. **Customer interaction** – this helps people to not only understand the customer's immediate needs but also to see the 'bigger picture'. Customer interaction should be facilitated by:

- orientation and focus of people's roles to be customer centric
- encouraging visits by the customer and to the customer
- trusting employees to interact with their customers.

D. **Supervision** – this includes orientation to policy and procedure, explanation of expectations, day-to-day monitoring and feedback on performance and assistance in small-scale problem-solving. Effective supervision includes:

- close proximity between the two parties and frequent interactions
- an environment conducive to constructive feedback and questioning
- a sense of trust and credibility between the two parties.

E. **Mentoring** – differs from supervision in that the mentor is not responsible for the individual's output, hence no expectations or monitoring. Mentoring is often more about longer-term issues for the individual rather than the day to day. This is often an informal arrangement at the choice of both parties. To encourage mentoring on this basis the organizations should:

- acknowledge expert employees
- promote a culture where people are encouraged to seek out and spend some time with each other, mentoring and being mentored.

F. **Shift change** – the study was exclusively engaged with manufacturing employers and hence this element is very sector specific. To translate it to a wider audience it relates to a transition period where one team or individual hands over the reins to the next in the process. To make this effective as a learning opportunity (as well as to improve productivity), it is important to:

- allow adequate time for the handover
- allow and encourage some personal interaction as well as purely productivity-related aspects
- have a common objective (rather than a competing one) between the parties.

G. **Peer-to-peer communication** – this includes the goal/work-orientated interactions but also, importantly, the social interactions (water-cooler chats, social meetings, 'gossip') as well. In order to maximize the learning value of this the organization should:

- provide spaces and opportunities for people to meet and chat
- trust that this is the valuable activity of networking rather than seeing it as 'notworking'.

H. Cross-training – this covers both individuals learning the other roles in their own area and individuals spending time learning about other elements and functions within their organization. Both add value since the former multi-skills each individual employee and the latter improves the understanding and commitment to the bigger picture. Effective informal cross-training requires the organization to allow time and resources to this activity (to the learner and the 'provider').

I. Exploration – this is the process whereby individuals initiate self-directed study or seek out resources that will help them to learn. To maximize this the organization should:

- recognize and encourage personal reflection
- provide trust, time, opportunities and resources to people to stretch their horizons, through secondments, projects and 'acting rank'
- be tolerant (within reason) of mistakes and errors; using them as learning opportunities rather than blaming opportunities
- allow, encourage or provide access to resources for people to explore and learn.

J. On-the-job (OJT) training – this is where a peer trains a newbie into their role. 80 per cent of the respondents reported that they learned from their peers in contrast to only 29 per cent from their manager/supervisor. On top of that, 81 per cent of people reported that they enjoyed the role of training a newbie. To maximize the value of OJT there needs to be:

- tolerance for mistakes during the learning period
- sufficient time given to both parties
- amendment of productivity targets for the 'trainer'
- clear learning/training goals for both parties
- an appropriate level of challenge.

K. Documentation – traditionally, documentation is a management responsibility, but the study found that all individuals gained from taking responsibility for documentation of their own and their team's performance. Producing other documentations such as user manuals, standard operating procedures, newsletters and instruction sheets also helped people to develop new skills as well as to become more familiar with bigger picture issues.

Clearly to do this people need to have the resources and recognition as well as management trust and tolerance.

L. **Execution of one's job** – this is so obvious that it almost belies consideration! But to maximize informal learning AND productivity the study identified some critical elements to this apparently mundane aspect:

- an appropriately stretching challenge!
- employee empowerment to solve problems themselves (with support but without having the problem taken away)
- encouragement to improve job processes.

M. **Site visits** – the study looked only at visits to customer sites to see the products in use. Obviously, one can also consider visits to suppliers and even benchmarking visits to best practice organizations. The important elements for exploiting these are:

- frequency and quality of the visits
- opportunity to see the products/best practices/raw materials in use in the 'real world'
- support to reflect on, implement and integrate ideas gained from the visits.

So much for the study, what can you do about it to make informal learning really happen?

Each of the 13 elements listed above includes the bullet points critical to success. By seeking every opportunity to initiate each of the elements you provide the raw materials for learning, by putting the bullet-pointed facets into place you maximize the learning and the productivity of each element. Job done!

So what are the big takeaways here?

- **Tell people about this study; not the training department or L&D function, but your staff and peer managers/leaders.** You will see that most of the enablers of informal learning are in the hands of the line management and the senior management of the company, rather than the HR function.
- **Look at your team (and your own situation).** What opportunities exist today for informal learning?

- **Next time you are writing or reviewing a person's annual appraisal, and you are thinking about their development over the next period, remember that there are 13 options listed above.** You can use any of these (or even all of them) before you start looking for a training course.

Source

eric.ed.gov/?id=ED461754

See also

Chapter 6 – As a leader, it is a matter of priorities

Chapter 26 – Learning; it's a generational thing

Chapter 31 – Meetings (n); Events where people get together (eventually) and waste a lot more time than they need to

Chapter 34 – Talent management – have you got your EVP right?

Chapter 38 – Learning from successful change

28 WHAT HAPPENS WHEN YOU (OR SOMEONE YOU MANAGE) MAKE DECISIONS UNDER PRESSURE?

It may be that when the going gets tough, the tough get going, but they may well go in the wrong direction if they wait for the going to get tough before plotting their course

Many studies over many years have shown that stress influences people's performance. Much of this research has focused on how stress affects memory, but it was clear that stress also affected emotional reaction, decision-making and other behaviours.

Research in 2012, by Mara Mather and Nichole Lighthall of the University of Southern California, examined the impact of stress solely on decision processes. It revealed two important findings:

1. Acute stress encourages the selection of previously rewarding outcomes but also impairs the rejection of previously negative outcomes.
2. Acute stress magnifies differences between men and women with regard to the strategies used to take risk-related decisions; men take more risk and women take less risk under stress.

Both these findings are based not just on observed behaviours but also on chemical analysis of different brain actions and reactions to decision-making in stressful situations. This chapter will not attempt to detail the 'dopaminergic reward-processing brain regions', the 'striatum, especially the nucleus accumbens' or the 'orbitofrontal cortex'. Neither will it attempt to make sense of the procedures that require people to be 'injected with a radiotracer' allowing researchers to observe the 'activity of specific neurotransmitters' in their subjects' brains via 'positron emission tomography'.

The report quotes two behavioural studies carried out under experimental conditions where the decisions involved selecting a cue that would give either a rewarding outcome or a negative outcome. The two studies used rather different stressors on the subjects: one required them to immerse their hands in iced water, providing a physical stressor, and the other required them to speak in public and at the same time carry out mental arithmetic.

A control group, unstressed, was also used in both studies.

Keep doing what you've been doing

The stressed group showed a marked inclination to take decisions that provided the same rewards that they had chosen when not stressed, in other words their judgement became more impaired and they were more likely to simply continue to do what they were used to doing.

Particularly interestingly, when the reward was food related, they continued to choose the food reward even when sated, whereas the unstressed group avoided this 'gluttony'.

There was no difference between males and females in this set of tests, just between the control groups and the stressed groups.

Venus and Mars divide

Another experiment referred to in the report indicates a gender divergence under stress in decision strategies.

In this research the subjects had to choose between:

- safer options: that offer lower potential gains, but also lower losses, and
- riskier options: higher potential gains, but also higher losses.

Study participants were tasked with inflating a series of balloons shown on the computer screen, the larger a balloon got, the more it was worth to the participant. Conversely, as the balloon got larger there was an increased risk of it popping, reducing its value to zero.

To maximize the value of their balloons, participants had to choose when to 'cash in' each balloon. Risk-taking is therefore simply defined by the number of pumps the subject put into each balloon before deciding to cash it in.

Half of the participants underwent the iced water stressor before undertaking the task, half didn't and were the control group.

The study's findings were that:

- Females took less risk on individual balloons than males whether stressed or not.
- Females who were stressed took less risk on individual balloons than females who were not stressed.
- Males who were stressed took greater risk on individual balloons than men who were not stressed
- Females who were stressed took considerably less risk than males who were stressed, by a factor of around 30 per cent!

It is worth noting however that the risk-taking in stressed males did not reach a level of diminishing returns; they were therefore able to earn more reward than their female counterparts.

This exercise was then replayed, but this time the reward was for speed; a constant amount of time was allowed and the more balloons each subject inflated, the more they 'earned'. In this iteration, stress did not affect the number of pumps per balloon that participants made (risk-taking) but, instead, affected their decision speed and number of balloons cashed in.

In the control group, males and females each cashed in 13 balloons on average.

In the stressed group males cashed in an average of 19 balloons and females only 7!

In this study the participants were actually in an fMRI scanner and the researchers observed consistent differences in the brain activity between the males and the females of each stressed and control group.

There is the science, but so what? What can you do with it as a leader/manager?

The laboratory studies reviewed here provide evidence that stress affects decision-making and risk-taking. Managers and staff members are often under conditions of stress. So:

First, be consciously aware that stress has an effect on people's decision-making capacity; they are more likely to go for previously successful options. This reduces creative problem-solving, entrenches the status quo and is more likely to lead to organizational inertia at the very time when new thinking is required. On the other hand, it can make people repeat previous errors, again at just the time when fresh approaches are appropriate.

Either way, one person taking sole responsibility for decision-making, while under stress is a recipe for danger! If that one person is you as a leader... need one say more?

Second, be aware of the differing effect that stress has on people's attitude to risk. It changes it. This makes objective risk assessment far more important than it might otherwise be. It also suggests that risk assessment carried out, if possible, at a time clear of stress is better than risk assessment carried out under stressful conditions. Clearly this is not always possible; risk assessments often have to be carried out in the heat of the moment. If this is the case try to get people who are not under the same stress to carry out the risk assessment.

Be aware of the gender differences in risk attitude and decision-making under stress. Take them into account when allocating decision-making tasks. That is not to say that you should allocate tasks according to gender, but to ensure mixed, and therefore more likely to be balanced, teams to consider decisions.

Be suspicious of decisions made by single-gender teams, but do remember that, in the tests, the males' more risky strategies didn't result in failure.

So what are the big takeaways here?

- **Challenge people in your team about their attitude to risk taking when under stress** (don't actually challenge while they are under stress but talk about their stress-time attitudes at a safer time).
- **Think about how you allocate decision-making and risk-related management tasks to people when the going gets tough...** or do you keep it to yourself? Think about who you might turn to to help you balance your attitude to risk and decision-making under pressure. Try to take major decisions early enough to avoid the stress pressure associated with leaving the decision-making until the last minute. Encourage your people to do likewise.
- **Remember that this isn't gender stereotyping;** it is backed up by genuine neuroscience.

Source

Mather, M. & Lighthall, N. R. (2012), 'Risk and Reward are Processed Differently in Decisions Made Under Stress', *Current Directions in Psychological Science*, Vol. 21 Issue 1 pp 36–41
www.usc.edu/projects/matherlab/pdfs/MatherLighthall2012.pdf

See also

Chapter 8 – 'What's "luck" got to do with it?'

Chapter 10 – The five-step ladder to increased success

Chapter 25 – Is teamwork always the answer?

Chapter 35 – 'Trust me, I'm a manager'

29 IS GETTING ENGAGED REALLY WORTH THE EFFORT?

This is the 'sequel' to Chapters 9 and 16... it reinforces and supports the importance of winning the hearts and minds of your people

'Engaging for success: enhancing performance through employee engagement' is a whopping 157 pages long. It is a Crown copyright document and can be downloaded free of charge from the 'Source' reference at the end of this chapter.

It is the work of David MacLeod and Nita Clarke, in response to a request by John Hutton, the UK's Secretary of State for Business. They commenced work in the autumn of 2008 to 'take an in-depth look at employee engagement and to report on its potential benefits for companies, organizations and individual employees'. The report was published in July 2009.

It should be recommended reading for every manager, leader or management or leadership aspirant in the world.

It doesn't record a new experiment or survey, but it collates and codifies a myriad scholarly works from around the world. The authors make it quite clear that no single one of these works is individual, exclusive or irrevocable proof, but that as a body of work, by a wide range of academics and business minds, they present very compelling evidence that, yes, employee engagement is worth it.

This chapter doesn't aim to summarize the entire report. It only aims to cover Chapter 2: The Case for Employee Engagement – The Evidence.

The chapter opens by accepting that many critics of the concept of employee engagement point out that there are organizations where no effort is made to engage employees and they are clearly disengaged, but, in spite of this, the organization thrives and prospers. This is a truism. As the authors point out, there is also a significant body of evidence that clearly suggests that those organizations that do actively engage their employees see, in the case of commercial, profit-making firms, an improvement in their financial results and, in the case of public sector and not-for-profit outfits, an improvement in their service levels and efficiency.

The commercial sector

Engagement and income

A global study by Towers Perrin in 2006 covered 664,000 employees from 50 companies, representing a range of different profit-making industries.

- ✓ Companies with a highly engaged workforce improved operating income by 19.2 per cent over a 12-month period
- ✗ Companies with low engagement scores saw operating income decline by 32.7 per cent over the same period
- ✓ Those companies with high engagement scores demonstrated a 13.7 per cent improvement in net income growth
- ✗ Those with low engagement saw net income growth decline by 3.8 per cent.

Engagement and employee sick days

A 2006 meta-analysis by Gallup looked at 23,910 commercial business units and found that:

- ✓ More highly engaged employees take an average of 2.7 days per year
- ✗ Disengaged employees take an average of 6.2 days per year.

Engagement and staff turnover

Development Dimensions International (DDI) reported in 2005 that in a Fortune 100 manufacturing company:

- ✗ Staff turnover in low engagement teams averaged 14.5 per cent

✓ In high engagement teams it was 4.8 per cent.

Engagement and absenteeism
('Absenteeism' is unauthorized sick days, 'throwing a sickie', unconfirmed compassionate leave, lateness.)

That same DDI study found that:

✗ In low engagement teams absenteeism hovered around 8 per cent
✓ But was only 4.1 per cent in high engagement teams.

Nationwide Building Society has a sophisticated approach to measuring engagement and comparing it to other measures on performance.

✓ They have calculated that if all their retail areas brought their engagement scores up to those in the top third, and there was a corresponding improvement in the absentee rates, this could represent a financial saving of £800,000 per annum.

Engagement and risk
Nationwide found that on a risk scale of 0-30, where 0 might be described as 'take no risk at all', and 30 might be a 'devil-may-care attitude to risk'...

✓ Highly engaged staff score 15
✗ Staff with low engagement score 27

Engagement around the world in the same organization
Standard Chartered Bank researched their branches in Hong Kong and Ghana between 2002 and 2004 and found that:

✓ Branches where employee engagement was high achieved 16 per cent higher profit margin growth than branches where employee engagement was low
✓ and had 46 per cent lower voluntary turnover.

The studies listed above all relate to commercial organizations and the value to them of higher employee engagement, but what of the public sector?

The public sector

Engagement and pride in the 'badge'

A 2006 survey carried out by Ipsos MORI of staff in UK local councils, found that:

✓ where the council was rated 'excellent' by the Audit Commission, there was a higher level of 'staff advocacy'; that phenomenon where staff were proud enough of their employer to speak highly about it to others outside.

Engagement and education results

The results of a schools survey by West Berkshire Council, as presented to the MacLeod report authors in February 2009, found:

✓ Significant correlations between school staff engagement and pupil attainment.

Engagement and productivity, motivation and stress reduction

Beverly Alimo-Metcalfe, professor of leadership at Bradford University, has carried out a three-year longitudinal study of 46 mental health teams working in Britain's NHS. Her study, published in 2008, indicates that

✓ a culture of engagement predicted performance. *'We were able to provide evidence that engaging leadership does, in fact, predict productivity. We also found that this style of leadership increases employees' motivation, job satisfaction and commitment, while reducing job-related stress. Leadership skills alone do not have such a transformational effect.'*

Engagement and service delivery

In 2006 South Tyneside Council committed to improving and maintaining high levels of employee engagement; positive results by 2008 included:

✓ Growing satisfaction by residents with South Tyneside as a place to live: up 4 per cent to 77 per cent

✓ A total of 77 per cent of residents felt that the council was working to make the area safer, up 12 per cent since 2006.

And finally... Engagement through wellbeing during a period of downsizing

A four-year longitudinal study, by Professor Sharon Parker from Sheffield University (published in 1997), showed that despite downsizing and increased work requirements there was no overall decrease in wellbeing from before, to after.

The potentially detrimental effect of increased demands appeared to have been offset by initiatives introduced as part of the downsizing strategy. The study showed that though downsizing and higher demands on the workforce are usually associated with poorer wellbeing, increases in participation can offset this, maintaining staff wellbeing and contributing to higher engagement and performance.

So what are the big takeaways here?

- **Spread the word about these study results;** engagement is not just a nice-to-do when you can afford it, nor is it an only-to-be-done-to-increase-profits. Quote the numbers... they speak for themselves.
- **Make engagement a priority for you and your organization...** it may not show results on the balance sheet in the next financial quarter, but it will bring across-the-board benefits for all the stakeholders in your sector.
- **Remember that there are many ways of measuring engagement,** and many facets that contribute to improving it or reducing it. There is no silver bullet, it requires consistent effort.

Source

www.engageforsuccess.org/ideas-tools/employee-engagement-the-macleod-report/#.VL9NrmByapo

See also

30 MANAGING THE MILLENNIALS... SOME NEW CHALLENGES

Dinosaur managers (and leaders) lead as if they are living in the past... but if their followers are living in the present there could be lost opportunities

The millennial generation, Generation Y; the people born post-1982 are stereotypically different from the previous generations. By 2025, three-quarters of the global workforce will be millennials, but how much have organizations changed their working practices in response to the generational difference? How much do they need to change? It isn't likely that the existing world of work is going to change the ingrained characteristics of an entire generation.

In January 2014, Bentley University in Boston, New England, created The PreparedU Project to 'spur a national dialogue and uncover solutions' to the differences between millennials and what employers are currently geared up to do.

They ran their study in two phases:

First, they conducted the 'Millennial Preparedness Study'. This looked at what:

- corporate recruiters
- business executives
- parents
- higher education leaders, and
- millennials themselves

... thought about the preparedness gap that Generation Y faces in today's workplace.

Then they asked 1,031 millennials, ages 18 to 34, what they think about their own preparedness for their professional life and what they wanted out of their career.

1. 50 per cent of millennials say the main reason people their age are unprepared for their first job is a poor work ethic. However, 89 per cent of them admit to regularly checking work email after work hours, while 37 per cent say they always do. When asked what would make them more productive their responses included: more flexible work hours; more remote working; more frequent, shorter breaks during the working day; and fewer/shorter meetings... everyone wants those things to make them more productive.
2. The typical, traditional 9-to-5 schedule doesn't appeal to many millennials: 77 per cent say flexible hours would make the workplace more productive for people their age. This may be part of a wider shift towards a more equitable work/life balance; according to Aaron Nurick, professor of management and psychology at Bentley, since the 1970s people have been pushing for more workplace flexibility. It's to be expected that the younger generation is on the edge of this trend. Obviously, an organization's consumers must be taken into account and they will ultimately determine to what extent flexible work schedules become viable. New, more mobile technology already allows some of us to work from anywhere at any time.
3. Older generations tend to think millennials favour texting and social media for all their communication, but:

   • 51 per cent of millennials say they would rather communicate with a work colleague in person
   • 19 per cent by email
   • 14 per cent by text
   • 9 per cent live phone call
   • 7 per cent online 'chat' or similar.

There are gender differences, however; male millennials are slightly more likely to prefer speaking to a colleague in person (56 per cent) than women (48 per cent), while women tend to rely more on email for communication (23 per cent) than men do (13 per cent).

However, it does also depend on the topic of the communication; Millennials crave validation of their outputs; praise and comment... this they prefer to seek out face to face. They also recognize their need for clear direction and expectations from their manager/client and prefer to do this face to face as well.

txt is da bst way to chat to m8s

4. Millennials may be more 'responsible' than most of the older generations imagine. When offered a choice between two otherwise identical jobs, 96 per cent of them said that good healthcare benefits would be an important factor in their decision.

5. Millennials are often perceived to lack loyalty. But 80 per cent of millennials believe they'll work for four or fewer companies in their career. A surprising 16 per cent anticipate staying in the same career for their entire working life. This is a belief and it is at odds with the current statistics; a 2010 study by the Bureau of Labor Statistics in the USA found that, on average, people had 11 different jobs in their career. This figure was pretty stable regardless of educational attainment, ethnicity or gender, so the millennials' hope for stable employment would seem to be at odds with the reality of the labour market they are entering.

6. Millennials want to work for organizations they deem ethical, but they still have a strong desire for regular salary increases. 79 per cent expect a pay rise every year.

7. Millennials view career success differently than their parents do. Rather than striving for the CEO spot, 66 per cent of millennials would like to start their own business and 37 per cent want to work on their own. This may account for some of the findings in '5' above. When you run your own business you can stay with the same employer all your life, though you may have a different client every day.

So there are the findings of the study, what can you do to take advantage of them to get the best out of the millennials of Generation Y?

'Growing up in a world of technology and instant gratification, they are interested in putting in extra effort, but only if they can clearly see the benefits,' said Susan Brennan of Bentley University, commenting on the report. This means that when managing this group you need to be constant and consistent in reminding them of the benefits they gain; you may not be able to say: 'Do this well and there is a promotion in it for you' or 'Do this well and there is a bonus in it for you' but try to verbalize the WIIFY (What's In It For You) on an almost daily basis. Use some of the developmental suggestions covered in Chapter 26; for example, putting people on exciting projects as a reward is a great way to motivate millennials.

Encourage and support extracurricular social responsibility, if possible, in work-paid time. This can be used as a reward or simply to support the millennial's desire for #6 above. It is also an opportunity for the organization to generate good PR, so it has a payback to the employer as well as the employee.

Get out of your office and talk to people rather than falling back on email. Especially note the important things for face-to-face communication; directions and validation, the two 'end points' of good performance management. But note that millennials are already predisposed to dislike meetings (they probably learned that from their parents' moans and groans) so try to improve your meeting management skills. (See Chapter 31.) Use the Internet technology available for meetings so that more work can be done remotely. This will kill two birds with one stone.

Encourage people, where possible, to have a micro-business of their own as well as a job working for you. Many organizations already allow this and some actively encourage it; so long as the individual's micro-business isn't directly competing with you (or reliant on stealing and selling your office supplies), there are several benefits to this policy. First, it encourages the development of a higher level of commercial acumen than you may be able to offer in the job description. Second, it will probably 'sort the wheat from the chaff'... most start-ups fail, so it will prove that being your own boss and running your own business is not as easy as it looks. This might both prevent the good people from leaving you and prevent them from taking the big leap to a non-salaried role and failing spectacularly.

Where possible, provide as flexible a workplace as you can. Challenge the old notions of the strictly 9-to-5, operate a more ROWE type of environment (see Chapter 32).

So what are the big takeaways here?

- **The millennial generation is actually not that different from their parents and grandparents once you get below the surface,** so next time you hear one of your colleagues moaning about the 'youth of today', share the findings of this report.
- **Improve your management of meetings;** be more accurate in your directions and be more giving of genuinely constructive feedback. This will not only help the millennials immensely, but everyone else as well... including you!
- **Remember that millennials are people too...** to treat them differently may well be to discriminate unfairly, either against them or against your older team members.

Sources

www.slideshare.net/BentleyU/preparedu-the-millennial-mind-goes-to-work-41415813

www.mindflash.com/blog/2011/05/how-many-jobs-do-americans-hold-in-a-lifetime

See also

Chapter 4 – I read it, but what the heck did it mean?

Chapter 10 – The five-step ladder to increased success

Chapter 23 – We're working nine to five – it's no way to make a living

Chapter 30 – Managing the millennials... some new challenges

Chapter 31 – Meetings (n); Events where people get together (eventually) and waste a lot more time than they need to

Chapter 32 – ROWE, ROWE, ROWE your boat!

Chapter 34 – Talent management – have you got your EVP right?

31 MEETINGS (N); EVENTS WHERE PEOPLE GET TOGETHER (EVENTUALLY) AND WASTE A LOT MORE TIME THAN THEY NEED TO

Whether you run or attend meetings you can probably improve their productivity... if you don't believe that, read on

More and more people are spending more and more of their time in meetings than ever before. An MIT survey in 2007 by Rogelberg, Scott and Kello of 1,900 business leaders revealed that they are spending 72 per cent more of their time in meetings than they did in 2002 and 49 per cent of them expected their time in meetings to increase.

Another survey reported that:

- most professionals believe >50 per cent of time spent in meetings is wasted
- >90 per cent of people admit to daydreaming in meetings
- 73 per cent have brought in and done other work in meetings to pass the time productively
- And, amazingly, 39 per cent admit to having fallen asleep in a meeting!

Everyone has advice on how to make meetings more productive but there is actually little empirical research to back up much of this advice.

One useful study into meetings and meeting management was published in 2009 by Kelly A. Lambing, who is research committee chair of the St. Louis Institute for Internal Auditors and team leader, Internal Audit Services at Anheuser-Busch Companies, Inc.

108 audit professionals completed the survey, which assessed a range of aspects of meetings and meetings management. The survey asked not only for the reasons why unproductive meetings were unproductive, but also why, in the respondents' opinions, the productive meetings were so much more productive.

The survey group came from a pretty wide range of levels within the hierarchy:

Professional	15%
Senior professional	26%
Professional team leader	10%
Manager/senior manager	31%
Director/partner & above	18%

The causes of failure

Respondents were asked to rate a series of factors that contributed to their meetings being unproductive and the following trends were noted:

1. **Diversions:** People ranked having too many diversions to the focus of the meeting as being the definite and most likely factor for unproductive meetings.
2. **Objective not met:** Respondents indicated that not reaching the objective was the third-highest definite factor and second-highest likely factor causing meetings to be judged a waste time.
3. **Ineffective meeting chair:** The chair not fulfilling their responsibilities for controlling and directing the meeting was cited as the second-highest definite factor and fourth-highest likely factor for unproductive meetings.
4. **Too heavy an agenda:** Finally, respondents cited having too many agenda items to cover in the allotted time was the third-highest response as a likely factor for unproductive meetings.

The causes of success

People were also asked to consider the meetings they considered productive and to rate the factors that made them so. The results of this question did not reveal concise elements, but do provide an insight into the factors of productive meetings.

1. **On-track with agenda:** People indicated that staying on track with a given agenda was a definite factor in making meetings successful.
2. **Purpose:** Attending a meeting that was immediately relevant to their job duties was the second-highest definite factor to productive meetings.
3. **Effective chairing:** Effective chairing was cited as the third-ranking definite factor to productive meetings.
4. **Concise agenda:** Having a concise agenda was the highest likely factor to predicate success.
5. **Objective met:** Feeling as if the objective was met was the second most likely factor.
6. **Group size and venues:** Finally, having an appropriate number of attendees and good venues/technology tied for being the third-highest likely factor.

The report recognized that there are fundamentally two types of meeting and the two have rather different dynamics.

There are meetings where the objective is the passage of information but no real feedback or engagement is sought from the 'audience'. And there are meetings where decisions need to be made, usually on the back of some information passing at or before the meeting. The respondents in this survey reported that the split between the two was almost half and half and the feedback they gave referred to both types. However, the most significant failing in decision-making meetings was for the decision to be rescheduled (for any of the aforementioned reasons) to a future meeting. Of course anecdotal evidence suggests that if this can happen once it can become a serial occurrence and the decision can be delayed again and again and the meetings simply become a talking-shop.

The beauty of this study is that it goes straight on to make recommendations for improving the effectiveness of meetings. Here is a summary of the recommendations.

- Develop a brief and to-the-point objective for the meeting.
- Evaluate from this whether a meeting is required to achieve the objective.
- Decide who needs to input to this objective. There should be fewer than 15 people working together on any decision-making meetings, while information-sharing can be as large as needed… if someone isn't needed, don't invite them.
- Include your objective in the meeting invitation.
- Produce an agenda; keep it to less than one-page and head it with the objective to keep it in focus. Allocate time to each agenda item while remembering that the ideal meeting length is between 45 minutes and an hour and a half. Assign around 10 per cent of the time to introducing the meeting, 85 per cent for the achievement of the objective and 5 per cent to conclude it.
- Distribute the agenda at least one day in advance of the meeting; be clear what preparation people need to do before they turn up.
- Introduce the meeting and attendees, repeat the objective and set expectations for the meeting attendees with regard to behaviours (e.g. questions and comments) and timings.
- Actively lead the meeting by keeping the agenda on track. If it is a particularly formal meeting or a contentious decision you may want to have a neutral facilitator/chair.
- Stop any diversions or new topics. If they have value, 'park' them on a visible list so they can be addressed outside/after the current meeting.
- Summarize each item as it is completed, ensuring that actions and timescales are clearly allocated to a responsible person.
- If appropriate, meeting minutes should follow the flow of the agenda and include attendees, discussion, decisions and actions agreed-upon. They should be issued within 24 hours to attendees and other stakeholders.
- Periodically, survey meeting attendees' opinions on meeting productivity to help maintain and improve the effectiveness of meetings. (Page 18 of the study contains an excellent tool for this really useful activity.)

The report goes on to look at the use of technology, teleconferencing, video-conferencing and 'web-hosted interactive media' as alternatives to face-to-face meetings. The technology of 2015 is massively different from the time the report was compiled in 2008 so we will not look into that aspect here.

So what are the big takeaways here?

- **If you come out of a meeting feeling that it just wasted an hour or more of your life,** don't just put up with it, tell the meeting chair about this chapter. Especially bearing in mind that several other people probably felt the same as you did!
- **Take Lambing's work to heart.** Start following the advice and recommendations above; they are not too onerous and could save you and your team hundreds of unproductive hours per year.
- **Remember that meetings are vitally important to organizations** and they are also probably the single biggest time-waster of most people's lives!

Source

https://na.theiia.org/iiarf/Public%20Documents/Increasing%20 Meeting%20Effectiveness%20for%20Internal%20Auditors%20 -%20St.%20Louis.pdf

See also

Chapter 3 – It ain't what you say, it's the way that you say it

Chapter 4 – I read it, but what the heck did it mean?

Chapter 10 – The five-step ladder to increased success

Chapter 25 – Is teamwork always the answer?

Chapter 32 – ROWE, ROWE, ROWE your boat!

Chapter 36 – Stop paying attention to the PowerPoint® default settings!

Chapter 40 – You can NOT be serious!

32 ROWE, ROWE, ROWE YOUR BOAT!

Now is the time to try to break away from measuring, monitoring and rewarding time spent doing work, and start rewarding the achievement of results

As soon as we are born our lives are managed by the amount of time spent on doing things:

- We are expected to walk/talk/read by the time we reach a particular age
- We are expected to practise the piano for so many hours a day/ week
- We attend school for a given number of years.

This is then reinforced as we reach adulthood (another time-related milestone).

- Our degree at university takes a certain amount of time to obtain regardless of how much work we put in or how bright we are
- Our wages or salaries are calculated by the hour/day/week/ month almost in spite of our productivity
- People judge us by how many years' experience we have, even if by law they aren't technically allowed to
- Pay reviews are often incremental, based on number of years' service, albeit that part of this is to handcuff us to our current employer.

Many organizations are trying to find a way to break out of this culture; why? Because it predicates attendance rather than results and results are what keep commercial businesses running and public sector organizations serving the populations they support.

One apparently successful methodology to help achieve this change in focus is ROWE™ – Results-Only Work Environment.

Brainchild of Jody Thompson and Cali Ressler, of CultureRx, a ROWE™ changes the focus:

From...	To...
Culture of entitlement	Culture of opportunity
Focus on schedules and time off	Focus on work
Subjective conversations	Objective conversations
Individual focus	Team/organization focus
Time as the currency of work	Results as the currency of work
Freedom without accountability	Accountability first
Managers say: 'All hands on deck'	Results coaches foster: 'Everyone on point'
Manages flexibility (permission-based)	100% autonomous and accountable
No results? No more flexibility	No results? No job

Sounds good, but does it work?

CultureRx's website has a number of case studies to read; they range from family businesses to advertising agencies, accounting firms to consultancies – all claiming significant success as a result of the ROWE™ approach.

The difficulty (for this book) is that ROWE™ is a proprietary brand and relies on a specific client-focused 'formula', so how-to-do-it isn't an easy pick-up model.

However, if we assume that the proof of the pudding is in the eating, we can look at one of the case studies to see if the concept works.

In August 2011, 50 volunteers out of the 240-strong staff at Prairie Lakes Area Education Agency (PLAEA) in rural Iowa, USA, began to pilot a Results-Only Work Environment.

The PLAEA serves schools in 14 counties across 8,000 square miles with 30,000 students and 3,500 educational staff.

After piloting it for a year, the PLAEA was sufficiently impressed to roll it out to the rest of its employees. This was not during a period of economic success and easy decisions; PLAEA faced significant hiring and staff-retention challenges, due to the rural location and the bureaucratic nature of the role. The area was losing population and school enrolments dropped by around 10 per cent between 2005 and 2011. Education budgets are based on number of students, so budgets were falling, hampering recruitment and encouraging a focus on costs.

The 'test-pilots' started off by working together (in their specific work teams) to answer five fundamental questions:

1. What is our outcome?
2. Who is our target audience?
3. What activities will help us achieve that outcome?
4. What activities will NOT help us to achieve that outcome?
5. How will we measure success?

This focused their minds effectively and one of the most potent comments from the case study documentation is:

We are trying to block out the noise and clutter of all the things we used to ask people to do that did not lead to improved results for our students. We are moving to an environment in which we make all meetings optional; do not require people to update their calendars on a daily basis (they still keep one for themselves, because they know where they need to be to achieve their results) but rather focus on the work that needs to be done; and we are trying to involve more of our staff members in our Agency's leadership. We hope that the people closest to the decision impact will embrace this enhanced autonomy and decision-making authority – because we know that this will lead to a more effective and enjoyable work environment.

By making this change in focus the teams were able to produce some impressive sounding results:

'Our goal with our ROWE™ project was to increase reading accuracy rates....

We were able to get in there with students and teachers....

And it worked. Students raised reading accuracy scores and when we were done all of the students were reading above the 95th percentile.'

Unfortunately, the case study doesn't specify the starting point from whence the study began so though the comment was that 100 per cent of the students were in the 95th percentile by the end we don't know what amount of improvement this actually represents. However, we do know that the section concerned was the Special Educational Needs section, so it is fair to assume that the result was quite impressive.

Other benefits quoted without specific measurement are:

- Increased value to taxpayers as a result of the new focus on results
- Greater efficiency and productivity
- Easier talent attraction and better staff retention
- Elimination of non-productive meetings
- Improved clarity in goal-setting and measuring of outcomes.

The ROWE™ allowed staff to be more in control of their time and this is reported to have produced greater efficiency. Most of the staff spend a lot of their time out of the PLAEA's office, driving to schools and meeting with teachers and students. The ROWE™ created 'grown-up' work culture that allowed people to focus on results rather than face time. Each employee was trusted to take their own decisions about where they needed to be, and when.

This chapter doesn't intend to be a thinly veiled advert for CultureRx, but it is a quasi-scientific look at the movement away from the time-bounded culture and the benefits of focusing more on results as a way of engaging employees and empowering them to succeed at what they need to do. ROWE™ was a vehicle for achieving this and so is worth investigation.

So what can you do with this knowledge to improve your leadership and management of people and achieve results even when times are tough?

1. Focus on opportunities; these can be opportunities to improve the service the customer gets or opportunities for the employees to be more effective.
2. Meet with your people and ask them the five questions that appear early in this chapter. Explain the concept of a ROWE™ to them and ask if they'd value working this way.
3. Set good objectives with your people; these are objectives that focus almost exclusively on the needs of their customers, whether they are internal or external. Make sure that these are set, reviewed and measured regularly enough to make them meaningful; an annual target is all very well, but too far away. Quarterly, monthly or even weekly targets are more likely to be effective, so break the annual targets down.
4. Eradicate as many unnecessary meetings as you can and reduce reporting down as much as possible to be results focused.
5. Reduce your personal reliance on people's face time... working with the customer is more important than being seen in the office. Encourage others to follow you in this; it only needs one witty riposte of 'hello part-timer' to really cheese off the person who has been focusing on results and therefore not in the office.
6. Support people's empowerment and taking of this responsibility. If they need to have better technology in order not to have to come in for face-to-face meetings, then give them this technology.

So what are the big takeaways here?

- **Tell your people and your peers about the successes that organizations have had by focusing on results rather than timekeeping.** It is so obvious that many people actually miss it!
- **Take a critical look at your own objective-setting and measurement capability;** improve that and you'll improve your productivity.
- **Remember that presentism doesn't necessarily equate to success** and a lack of face time doesn't necessarily equate to slacking!

Source

Ressler, Cali & Thompson, Jody, *Why Work Sucks And How To Fix It: The Results-Only Revolution* (Portfolio, New York, 2008)

www.slideshare.net/eddodds/plaea-case-study

See also

Chapter 7 – 'An employee's workspace is his castle... or should be!'

Chapter 10 – The five-step ladder to increased success

Chapter 11 – To follow me they have to be able to see me, right?

Chapter 21 – Management and leadership... a hot topic! But for whom?

Chapter 29 – Is getting engaged really worth the effort?

Chapter 39 – Trust in your virtual team

33 FIND OUT WHAT YOUR FOLLOWERS THINK ABOUT YOU, AND TALK TO THEM ABOUT IT!

Listen to the grass roots grumbles as much or more than you listen to the boss's opinion of your success... the latter will follow the former

You get your annual appraisal from your boss. It is usually based predominantly on your attainment of targets; the 'what' you have achieved.

What the boss doesn't necessarily see is the detail of how you achieved it; you may be an absolute slave-driver, bullying and coercing your people to hit their targets and fulfil your needs. So long as you keep the boss happy everything else is irrelevant; you'll get a good appraisal and you'll rise up to the top of the pile.

You may know that your people think you are a slave-driver, and you may not care.

Or you may be kidding yourself that they are following you willingly when in actual fact they are following out of fear. They may not argue with you because they agree with you, or they may not argue with you because you write their annual appraisal and they don't want to bite the hand that feeds them.

So 'upward feedback' was invented to allow managers and leaders the power to see themselves as others see them. It is a potentially powerful tool in correcting or confirming a person's self-image.

The First Tennessee Bank in association with La Salle University undertook what is still the longest validated study of the effects of upward feedback processes; for five years, 252 managers were the target group of upward feedback from their staff. The outcomes of the study are enlightening in a number of ways.

Many organizations use 360-degree feedback tools as part of their performance management cycle. (360-degree feedback is marginally different to the upward feedback of the study but the outcomes are very similar.)

Some simply give the individuals the feedback and allow them to self-manage their reaction. However, Locke and Latham's 1990 study showed that feedback alone is not *often* adequate to lead to behavioural change. Instead it is the goals that people set in response to feedback that drives improvement and makes the whole exercise worthwhile. While some will effectively self-manage to some degree it seldom results in significant improvements.

Some demand that an individual discusses their feedback with their manager and then the two discuss the reasons for any feedback that suggests a need for behavioural change. This then leads to a consensus on how much the manager can and will change their future management style and specific behaviours.

Some expect that the individual discusses their feedback with an independent coach/mentor and agrees their reaction. This may work well when the individual accepts the feedback as accurate and fair, and wants to improve. The most obvious problem with this approach is that the individuals most in need of change are the ones least likely to accept the feedback and want to change.

The study in question, being upward feedback (rather than 360-degree) encouraged the individuals to meet and discuss the feedback, and their reaction to it, with the very people who had rated them – their direct reports.

The format of the feedback was constructed based on a series of in-house focus groups designed to identify the management behaviours believed to be appropriate to effective leadership, productivity and implementation of strategic business objectives. The assessment consisted of 29 behaviourally based items, each rated one a 1-to-5 scale from strongly agree to strongly disagree. The specific items covered included information-sharing, encouragement of team work, listening, positivity, continuous improvement, fairness, accessibility, recognition, support, empowerment, development of staff skills and acceptance of the feedback.

The results

The project clearly showed that managers initially rated 'poor' or 'moderate' showed significant improvements in their later upward feedback ratings over the five-year period.

Managers initially rated as 'excellent' maintained this rating over the five-year period.

Managers who did meet with their direct reports to discuss their upward feedback improved more than other managers who didn't.

Managers who didn't have these meetings every year improved more in the years when they did have these meetings with direct reports than in years when they did not.

So there is the data, what can you do about it to improve your management and leadership?

If your organization doesn't have an upward feedback process in place then create one yourself or with your team; the 29 questions they spent five years evolving are listed below to perhaps help you to generate a holistic approach.

1. My manager shares with me the information I need to do my job.
2. When I need it, my manager provides information about how I'm performing my job.
3. My manager has helped define the boundaries of empowerment for my position.
4. My manager promotes teamwork within our work unit.

5. My manager promotes teamwork between people in our work unit and people in other work units including those companywide.
6. My manager listens to my suggestions.
7. My manager keeps me informed on what the company is trying to accomplish.
8. My manager keeps me informed on what our work unit is trying to accomplish.
9. My manager involves our work unit in continuously improving the way we service our customers.
10. My manager encourages me to develop myself.
11. My manager makes sure I am trained to do my job.
12. My manager treats me with respect.
13. My manager lets me know when I've done a good job.
14. My manager presents a positive attitude towards the company and company policy.
15. My manager shares how Empowerment, Family Matters and Continuous Improvement initiatives can continue to improve our work unit's customer loyalty.
16. My manager works with me to ensure I understand the standards/goals on which my performance review will be based.
17. My manager is accessible for discussions.
18. My manager and I have discussed the knowledge, skills, and abilities that could affect my progress at this organization.
19. I have confidence in the fairness of my manager.
20. My manager makes sure that I present my views on my performance reviews.
21. My manager promotes a positive atmosphere.
22. My manager makes sure that I get the recognition for my performance.
23. Our work unit has plans in place for resolving customer problems.
24. My manager helps me understand our work unit's service approach.
25. If I thought I needed to go out on a limb to deliver excellent service, I am confident my manager would support me.
26. My manager works with me to help resolve conflicts between work and family/personal issues.
27. My manager coaches me on how I can continuously improve the service I provide to my customers.

28. My manager has held a feedback session concerning last year's Leadership Survey with our work unit.
29. Over the next 12 months, which one of the above items (1-28 above) should your manager work on the most?

If your organization already uses a 360-degree or upward feedback instrument, you can use that.

After the results are in, hold a meeting with the people who have provided feedback for you. Tell them upfront that the purpose is to help you to improve your management, not to chew them out for being mean or to thank them for being nice.

Don't ask for justification of their ratings; that will just open an argument. Probe to ensure that you understand the reasons behind their rating but avoid getting defensive.

Ask them what they think would be a better approach for you than the approaches you have been using so far. This will move you towards sensible action plans for improvement.

Outline SMART objectives for improvement and ask the team for their support, this means letting you know if you go off track (i.e. some at-the-time upward feedback). Then as you all return to BAU (Business As Usual) make sure you keep on top of the improvements.

> SMART = Specific, Measurable, Achievable, Relevant, Timebound (or similar; many organizations make changes to the words without changing the mnemonic).

So what are the big takeaways here?

- **Tell your people that you would actually appreciate upward feedback** and that you won't treat it as 'questioning the boss' or 'criticism' (so long as it is given at an appropriate time and place).
- **Stick to what you said in #1 above!**
- **Remember that if you don't know what you do badly you can't improve it.**

Source

https://www.tamu.edu/faculty/payne/PA/Walker%20&%20Smither%201999.pdf

See also

Chapter 2 – Do YOU really know what motivates your people?

Chapter 21 – Management and leadership... a hot topic! But for whom?

Chapter 25 – Is teamwork always the answer?

Chapter 31 – Meetings (n); Events where people get together (eventually) and waste a lot more time than they need to

Chapter 39 – Trust in your virtual team

34 TALENT MANAGEMENT – HAVE YOU GOT YOUR EVP RIGHT?

Just paying a (bigger) salary isn't the way to get and keep good people... there is a lot more to it than that

Talent management is seen by many as a key contributor to success. McKinsey's 2008 survey 'Why Multinationals Struggle To Manage Talent' cites the top third of organizations (in regard to their talent management) generate 39 per cent more profit per employee on average than the bottom third.

Towers Watson's Global Talent Management and Rewards Study 2012-13 took place between the end of April and the first week of June 2012. In total, 1,605 respondents participated in the survey; 40 per cent of the sample was from the Asia-Pacific region, including a very large sample from China. Europe, the Middle East and Africa contributed 26 per cent, North America 25 per cent and Latin America approximately 10 per cent.

Organizations had to meet a size threshold based on the number of employees or be part of a global organization. Two-thirds of the responses came from multinational organizations, and the remaining one-third were from large domestic organizations.

The industry representation was:

Manufacturing	31 per cent
Financial services	18 per cent
IT and Telecoms	16 per cent
Health care	12 per cent
General services	8 per cent
Wholesale and retail	8 per cent

| Energy and utilities | 6 per cent |
| Public sector | 2 per cent |

The study classified the employers according to the maturity of their EVP: their Employee Value Proposition.

The term refers to: *'the collective array of programs that an organization offers in exchange for employment. It defines "the give and the get" between company and worker, encompassing every aspect of the employment experience – from the organization's mission and values; to jobs, culture and colleagues; to the full portfolio of total rewards programs.'*

The classification of the employers according to their EVP was into four groups as follows:

Group 1. Do not have a total rewards approach or a formally articulated EVP.

Group 2. Have formally articulated an EVP and adopted a total rewards approach. There is a greater focus on an integrated strategy for managing rewards and talent, and they have stated objectives for each reward and talent management programme.

Group 3. Have effectively *communicated* their EVP to all employees and delivered on their EVP promises.

Group 4. Have *differentiated* their EVP from their competitors for talent (as opposed to their market competitors, though these may overlap) and have customized EVPs for critical workforce segments.

Results and findings

First, the bottom line:

- Global Group 4 employers are twice as likely to have financial performance substantially above their market competitors.
- In fast-growing economies the difference is a factor of two and a half times more likely.
- In developed economies it is around one and a half times.

This suggests that having a differentiated and customized EVP will predict higher financial success despite the economy in which the employer operates.

Next, let's look at some snapshots of the component parts; in all cases the comparison is the Group 4 with the Group 1:

- In developed economies Group 4 employers found it 6 per cent easier to recruit and 9 per cent less difficult to keep their good people.
- In fast-growing economies Group 4 employers find it 11 per cent easier to recruit good people and find 28 per cent less difficulty retaining their people than Group 1 employers.
- Across the board the Group 4 organizations are twice as likely to formally identify the employees whose skills are critical to the health of the organization.
- They are also almost twice as likely to formally identify the top performers.
- They are also almost twice as likely to formally identify the high potential people and nearly three times as likely to actually tell people that they are high potential employees.
- In Group 4 employers, people are nearly twice as likely to understand how their basic pay is determined.
- Employees in Group 4 organizations are nearly four times more likely to understand how they can personally influence their career future.
- And they are more than three times more likely to report that their line manager is effective at providing career management support as well as immediate line management supervision.
- They are 25 per cent more likely to think that the company's leadership development activity both supports the goals and strategy of the organizations and helps to create and maintain the desired culture in the organization.
- They are nearly two and a half times more likely to actually think that the company's performance management process helps to create a high-performing culture.
- They are 76 per cent more likely to report that the performance management system links an individual's salary to their actual performance.

As you can see, the study was wide ranging and comprehensive; these are just snapshots, perhaps about 30 per cent of the full findings of the report.

So there is the data, what value is this to you as a leader?

Only 18 per cent of the sample companies made it into the Group 4 category. Group 2 and 3 represented 26 per cent and 23 per cent respectively and the other 32 per cent of organizations fell into Group 1.

So if your organization is in Group 4 already you need to make sure that you stay in that group; it makes your life as a manager a heck of a lot easier. You can recruit and attract good people more easily, you can retain and motivate those people with less effort and this will have a beneficial effect on your financial results.

If your organization is in the Group 3 you only have two actions to go to move into Group 4 and reap the extra benefits for the relatively little effort.

- You need to benchmark your EVP against the organizations you compete with for talent. You may already be somewhere close to this already; if you feel that your salary offerings and benefits packages are 'competitive' then you are already carrying out some benchmarking. Close the circle by looking at the other aspects of the EVP; career support, management and leadership development and linking pay and benefits to individual performance.

If you are currently in Group 2 then you are on the way but you have a major communication task to fulfil to get to Group 3. It is now about making sure the workforce knows what you are doing and why.

If you are currently in Group 1, then you have a way to go. You have seen the benefits that this approach to EVP can take, both bottom line and in terms of easing day-to-day operations. Get coordinated talent management approaches going soon. Even if you are currently a small organization with plans to grow, it is much better to get the infrastructure in place now than to try to install it later into a larger organization, plus you can start to reap the rewards sooner.

So what are the big takeaways here?

- **Tell people about the benefits of a total rewards approach and a coordinated EVP.** It makes individuals' lives better and affects the bottom line as well.
- **Promote as much of it as you can in your own sphere of influence,** even if the organization won't adopt it overall. You can get some benefits for yourself and your team.
- **Remember that 'Talent Management' isn't just a euphemism for the graduate fast track programme...** there is way more to it than that, for everyone, not just the high potential people.

Sources

www.towerswatson.com/en-GB/Insights/IC-Types/Survey-Research-Results/2012/09/2012-Global-Talent-Management-and-Rewards-Study

www.talentnaardetop.nl/uploaded_files/document/2008_Why_multinationals_struggle_to_manage_talent_M.pdf

See also

Chapter 6 – As a leader, it is a matter of priorities

Chapter 21 – Management and leadership... a hot topic! But for whom?

Chapter 23 – We're working nine to five – it's no way to make a living

Chapter 24 – You don't have to love the quitters but at least listen to them

Chapter 29 – Is getting engaged really worth the effort?

Chapter 32 – ROWE, ROWE, ROWE your boat!

35 'TRUST ME, I'M A MANAGER'

To err is human, to regain public trust after you've erred just takes a bit more skill and knowledge (and guts)

The Institute of Business Ethics, the IBE, is a charitable organization based in London that aims to 'raise public awareness of the importance of doing business ethically, and collaborate with other UK and international organizations with interests and expertise in business ethics'. That is the theoretical bit of its objective.

On a more practical note it also 'helps organizations in the development, implementation and embedding of effective and relevant ethics and corporate responsibility policies and programmes. It helps organizations to provide guidance to staff and build relationships of trust with their principal stakeholders.'

'Trust'; generally people judge another party's trustworthiness according to a combination of three elements:

- **Ability or technical competence:** do we believe that they are able to deliver what they offer?
- **Benevolence:** do we believe that delivering it in the offered way is in their best interests?
- **Integrity:** do we believe in their honesty and fairness towards us?

If our overall judgement is positive, this increases our willingness to 'risk' dealing with them – to trust them, be they a person or an organization. This trust might take the form of:

- buying their products/services
- investing in their stock, or
- working for them.

But, should we have any reason to change our beliefs in any one of these attributes; Ability, Benevolence or Integrity, they lose our trust.

In February 2012 the IBE issued a publication that took six case studies and analysed them in some depth. Four of the case studies deal with organizations where:

- some people within each of these organizations had lost sight of the importance of ethical behaviour in their business transactions
- they had all been found out, publically
- they had all caused serious damage to their reputations and the trust that stakeholders had in them
- they had all had to put significant effort and resources into rebuilding that trust and they had all had to eat a lot of humble pie.

The publication's authors were Dr Graham Dietz, senior lecturer in human resource management and organizational behaviour at Durham University, UK, and Dr Nicole Gillespie, senior lecturer in management at the University of Queensland, Australia.

The organizations and their situations were:

- Siemens: Accused of systematic bribery in 2006, the scandal cost Siemens €2bn of fines, as well as 'repair' costs of around €63m
- The BBC: The 'phone-in' scandals in 2007-08. As a result the BBC had to pay to have 16,500 staff trained in ethics as well as paying a £50,000 fine
- BAE Systems: Persistent allegations of corruption in major sales resulted in £258m worth of fines and £1.7m bill for an internal audit and an undisclosed cost for training 88,000 staff
- Severn Trent Water: Found guilty of distorting performance data for the industry regulator Ofwat and fined £7.8m.

The report also covers another case study; one where the organization was proactive in identifying a problem and open about getting it sorted out:

Mattel, the toy giant, was faced with a series of quality issues after item sales in 2007, when two unrelated failures came to light in quick succession. They had sold 20 million potentially dangerous toys in 43 countries. The firm's proactive and honest approach has drawn widespread kudos and minimized the potential damage to their reputation (and of course the health of several million children).

The case studies support a series of actions (that had been initially described in the authors' previous 2009 publication 'Trust Repair After an Organization-Level Failure') that are commensurate with keeping or rebuilding trust in the event of a crisis:

Stage 1

Respond immediately, within 48 hours, of the incident coming to light. This comes in two forms: what to say and what to do.

> Coming to light can also mean internally. If a 'whistleblower' raises an issue to you through internal channels it is critical to be seen to be responding seriously and quickly. Failure to do so may be seen as intent to cover up the issue with the corresponding consequences

Say: Acknowledge the incident honestly and clearly, express the organization's regret in simple language (don't be 'mealy-mouthed'), announce the action you are taking immediately to mitigate the effects on relevant stakeholders, announce a full investigation and committed resources to prevent reoccurrence.

Do: what you just said!

Stage 2

Carry out or sponsor an accurate, systemic, inclusive and, if appropriate, independent diagnosis of the cause(s) of your organization's failure. This must demonstrate an appropriate sense of urgency and importance, and be actively transparent.

Stage 3

Carry out the deliberate actions arising from Stage 2. Again this comes in two forms; what to say and what to do.

Say: Apologize again (subject to culpability) and announce what reparations you are going to make (as appropriate). Announce the remedial action that you will put in long term.

Do: Derived from Stage 2, carry out a full implementation of remedial actions across the organization (as required), prioritizing according to failure type but with the caveat: 'Structural, procedural and cultural interventions should be adopted concurrently. For example, strengthening compliance monitoring and codes of conduct must be backed up (at the same time) with senior leaders' exhortations and training investment.'

Stage 4

Instigate a programme of accurate, systemic, multi-level, timely and transparent evaluation of the remedial actions.

This four-stage process sounds pretty straightforward and easy; however, the authors make it clear that the rebuilding of trust after a high-profile failure can take years rather than months. They also note that the effects on staff morale are potentially enormous; existing staff often carry a sense of shame for a long time. This period is extended when there are senior managers still in the organization who may have been tainted with suspicions of exhibiting, encouraging or turning a blind eye to unethical behaviour. 'Whistleblower amnesties' are often the most effective way to clear the air in this instance.

The report is predominantly advisory in its nature, and there are three particular paragraphs that every manager should keep in mind on the topic of trust and the organization:

'Guard against the downgrading or marginalization of trustworthiness and ethical procedures in the aggressive pursuit of quick growth. Too much growth, too fast, can weaken the robustness of organizational systems and values.'

If your organization is growing rapidly (or has grown rapidly) don't rest on your laurels and congratulate yourself on your success. Put in robust policies to make the ethical stance clear to all. Make time to ensure that everyone knows the policy and therefore what is and isn't acceptable. Ensure that in the focused pursuit of success, no one loses sight of what is right.

'Centralized corporate structures can paralyse local responsiveness, but de-centralized structures can lead to ungovernable local autonomy. There is a fine balance to be struck between trust and control.'

This is a challenge for any organization, large or small. 'Centralized' can mean physically in another city or country, or vested in another group or even person. If your organization appears to have either an iron grip or total autonomy, rather than a balance, there is a strong likelihood that some unethical behaviour is being demonstrated somewhere.

'In its live (Blue Peter) show on 27th November 2006, an "unavoidable technical difficulty" meant that no viewer could get through to the studio to take part in a charity phone-in competition. In the "blind panic" of a live broadcast, a junior employee – unbeknownst to the programme editor onsite – asked a child visiting the studio at the time to pretend to be the winner. Initially, the programme makers not only covered up what had happened, but the researcher responsible was apparently congratulated by the programme's editor for "keeping the show on the road".'

There is a fine line (and a grey one) between the use of initiative and a lack of integrity. Yes the show went out on TV without a hitch, but again that focus on success (bearing in mind that the BBC is not a commercial organization so the focus wasn't on profit) led to a 'little white lie'... even the 'good' lies are lies!

So what are the big takeaways here?

- If you hear one of your peers mention any form of unethical behaviour, challenge it. Share the costs of unethical behaviours as outlined in the early part of this chapter. Ask people what they'd say in court to justify their unethical action or their encouragement/condoning of it.

- **Make sure you are not encouraging or condoning unethical practice.** Make sure that your people know that you welcome a heads-up of any concerns where ethics are involved.
- **Remember that unethical behaviour bites your customer relationships, your shareholder relationships and your staff relationships.**

Source

www.ibe.org.uk/userfiles/op_trustcasestudies.pdf

See also

Chapter 1 – Spreadsheets alone do not a judgement make

Chapter 3 – It ain't what you say, it's the way that you say it

Chapter 4 – I read it, but what the heck did it mean?

Chapter 15 – Successful change begins with 'good' communication

Chapter 19 – The customer is always right… WRONG!

Chapter 25 – Is teamwork always the answer?

36 STOP PAYING ATTENTION TO THE POWERPOINT® DEFAULT SETTINGS!

Follow this advice to make a major improvement to your use of this potentially lethal tool

PowerPoint® – there can't be an office (except perhaps those owned by Apple) that doesn't have it. Most managers use it regularly. At some stage in our careers most of us suffer its appalling abuse to the level of 'Death By PowerPoint'.

To combat bad PowerPoint® habits there is a plethora of advice, but it is almost universally based on anecdotal evidence and personal opinion. There is hardly any actual scientific evidence for what makes good or bad PowerPoint®.

But there is some. Dr Joanna Garner (of Old Dominion University), along with Dr Sarah Zappe, Michael Alley, Lauren Sawarynski and Keri Wolfe (all of Pennsylvania State University, University Park) carried out a genuine lab condition test to compare two differing formats of PowerPoint® slide and the effect they had on the audience's ability to both understand and remember the information contained in the presentation.

The two formats were:

- the 'default' format, as embedded in the application: of a topic phrase headline supported by a bulleted list of subtopics or content

- the 'assertion-evidence' slide format: the heading is a succinct sentence assertion (in words) and the body of the slide supports that heading with *visual* evidence: photographs, drawings, diagrams, graphs, or words and equations *arranged in a visual way*.

The researchers noticed that the choice of format can affect the success of the presentation in three ways:

1. The format can affect the focus of the presenter (or designer) when deciding what to put on the slide. For example, an apparent difference is that if the assertion-evidence approach is taken the designer thinks of the presentation in terms of insights, features, results, and conclusions that the audience needs to know (the assertion), rather than topic phrases. The outcome of this is that the presenter is less likely to include extraneous details.
2. The choice of format of the slides can affect the delivery of the presentation. For instance, bulleted lists tend to encourage the presenter to turn to look at the screen (in the worst cases to actually read from the screen). The presenter breaks eye contact with the audience and sometimes looks as if he or she needs the visual aid more than the audience does.
3. Perhaps, most importantly, the format of the slides affects how much the listener understands and can later recall of the detail of the content of the presentation.

The research considered only this third effect.

The team carried out an experiment in which two different audiences listened to the same narrated presentation. Though the audio element was identical, they saw different types of slides.

One audience of 55 people saw 'traditional' topic-subtopic slides; the other, of 56 people, saw assertion-evidence slides. The stats looked like this:

Characteristic	Topic-Subtopic Slides	Assertion-Evidence Slides
Number of slides	11	10
Total number of words on slides	334	193
Average words per slide	30.4	19.3
Total length of presentation	6 m 17 s	6 m 17 s
Projected words per minute	53.2	30.7
Percentage of slides with relevant graphics	54.5	100
Number of slides with animations	0	9
Total number of words in spoken script	1,003	1,003
Spoken words per minute	159.6	159.6

As soon as the presentation was over, each audience was tested individually on both their understanding and their factual recall of the content.

A week after the presentations, the audiences had a further test on the content of the presentation. This unannounced test occurred in their normal environment.

The idea was to parallel the situation that occurs when any audience sees a presentation, although the audience had only the presentation to base their understanding of the information upon; they were not given the opportunity to ask questions or to request further details or reiteration.

Results

Comprehension

In the scores for comprehension of complex concepts immediately after the presentation the group who saw the assertion-evidence slides had a 16 per cent better result than the group who saw the topic-subtopic slides.

In the scores for comprehension of complex concepts one week after the presentation the group who saw the assertion-evidence slides had an 18 per cent better result than the group who saw the topic-subtopic slides.

Basic recall

Some less important statistics were verbally mentioned in the script of the presentation.

These were *included* as subtopics in the topic-subtopic slides but they did not appear on the visual of the assertion-evidence slides. The group who saw these statistics on the visual scored 30 per cent better than the group who only heard them.

Primary statistics appeared on both slide decks and the recall was identical between both groups on both tests.

Caveat

In spite of the scientific nature of this report, one may argue that 55 people (American university engineering students) are not representative of the world as a whole. However, put this with your own knowledge of being subjected to 400 slides one after the other, each with a title and a series of bullet points, and you would probably accept the report's findings as a breath of fresh air!

So there is the data; what can you do with it to improve your performance as a leader?

Next time you are called upon to present to a group, use the assertion-evidence approach for your visual aids. Look for good, appropriate visual representations of the subject; photos, drawings, graphics, clip art or graphs rather than words and numbers.

Avoid bullet points if you possibly can.

Rather than simply 'bullet pointing' words, if you have to use words then...

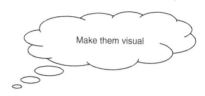

Think about, and plan, what you are going to SAY *before* you start trying to create the slides; this helps you to avoid falling into the topic-subtopic habit, which you might otherwise be drawn into.

People may find this a bit disconcerting at first; we are conditioned to PowerPoint® slides that look like this:

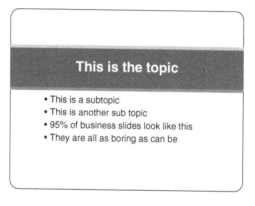

So they may be a bit shocked to see a slide that looks like this:

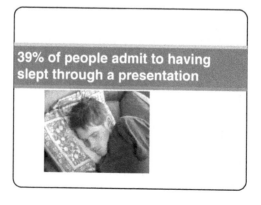

Recognize that this makes your job (at presenting) harder; the slides no longer act as a pauper's autocue and you need to find good graphic images that are free to use.

So what are the big takeaways here?

- **Tell your bosses about this research;** it may save you from being bored to death by poor visuals that you can't remember the day after. Tell your people about it so that they develop better PowerPoint® usage skills.
- **Change your own PowerPoint® tendencies; think graphically.**
- **Remember that it does mean extra work, so start preparing your next presentation early!**

Sources

www.writing.engr.psu.edu/research.html

www.engr.psu.edu/speaking/Visual-Aids.html

www.writing.engr.psu.edu/slides.html

See also

Chapter 4 – I read it, but what the heck did it mean?

Chapter 10 – The five-step ladder to increased success

Chapter 26 – Learning; it's a generational thing

Chapter 31 – Meetings (n); Events where people get together (eventually) and waste a lot more time than they need to

Chapter 40 – You can NOT be serious!

37 'SCIENCE, SCHMIENCE'... TAKE IT WITH A PINCH OF SALT

Beware this example of the fact that if you say it often enough everyone will believe it

If you have been in any management role in the developed world for more than a year you will doubtless have been told, read or seen a PowerPoint® slide that tells you that 70 per cent of all change programmes fail. You've probably seen it more than once. If you've been around for a bit longer you'll have seen it dozens of times. If you did an A level, a degree or higher in a business-related topic, you'll have seen it repeatedly.

Where does it originate from?

In 1993, James Champy and Professor Michael Hammer published a book: *Re-engineering the Corporation?*. This was based on research on Business Process Re-engineering initiatives in the last two decades of the 20th century in large organizations. It contained the statement:

'Sadly, we must report that... many companies that begin reengineering don't succeed at it... Our unscientific estimate is that as many as 50 per cent to 70 per cent of the organizations... do not achieve the dramatic results they intended.'

In 2000, researchers Michael Beer and Nitin Nohria published 'Cracking the Code of Change' in the *Harvard Business Review*. The sentence that grabbed people's attention was:

'The brutal fact is that about 70 per cent of all change initiatives fail.'

These two sources became widely read and quoted in academia to support and validate studies and reports into management practice and into change. They have also been widely used in management consulting, to help develop and sell change management ideas, theories and methodologies.

Thought leaders are still quoting them, for instance, Daryl Conner's 2012 blog post states:

'Change practitioners have some culpability for the atrocious 70 per cent failure rate of change initiatives.' (www.connerpartners. com/how-challenging-is-the-change/the-dirty-little-secret-behind-the-70-failure-rate-of-change-projects#sthash.bOgjhEXS.dpuf)

Ron Ashkenas wrote in the *Harvard Business Review* in 2013 that:

'... most studies still show a 60-70 per cent failure rate for organizational change projects – a statistic that has stayed constant from the 1970s to the present.' (https://hbr.org/2013/04/change-management-needs-to-cha)

However, as long ago as 1995, Professor Hammer wrote...

'Unfortunately, this simple descriptive observation has been widely misrepresented and transmogrified and distorted into a normative statement... There is no inherent success or failure rate for reengineering.'

There was *nothing* in 'Cracking the Code of Change' in the *Harvard Business Review* to actually support or justify the 'brutal fact' and no mention of where it came from.

The simple fact seems to be that once published by (a) reputable scientist(s), a statistic is accepted as being right. In Chapter 1 we looked at Aristotle's 'Model of Proof'. The ethos argument explains what has happened here; reputable people have made a statement and we generally accept that they know what they are talking about. When more reputable scientists repeat the initial assertion, usually in their work's references, the ethos strengthens.

'70 per cent' looks like a logical statistic. It has more logos potential than 'many', 'most' or 'a lot'. So added to the ethos, the assertion becomes even more likely to influence.

Once established the assertion gets repeated and repeated often enough it reaches a position where it is almost irrefutable.

Almost irrefutable.

More recently, there has been a significant amount of questioning regarding this '70 per cent of change initiatives fail' assertion:

www.bcs.org/upload/pdf/markhughes-060910.pdf

conversationsofchange.com.au/2013/09/02/70-of-change-projects-fail-bollocks1

Believers might accept that the 70 per cent statistic is unproven but claim that it is still quite viable, based on their own experience and or anecdotal evidence. These challenges, however, set out some very plausible arguments against the underlying likelihood.

It is important to note that these challenges are not dismissive of the need to plan and execute change sensibly. Their primary thrust is to attack the fear-mongering that is generated by the dilemma that such a massive likelihood of failure may engender; in other words, to dilute the pathos argument (back to Aristotle again). Under the pressure of a clear need to do something different, but faced with the choice between 'fail by stagnation' and 'fail by attempting to change', it is hard to make a rational decision (see Chapter 28).

Ok, that pooh-poohs the so-called scientific evidence; what can you do with this new knowledge that the old knowledge was dodgy?

When someone quotes this 'fact', ask them why they believe it. Have they checked any empirical research? Have they questioned it at all; what defines a change programme or reengineering?

What defines success? What effect does this statistic have on their approach to instigating or managing change in the real world?

Don't repeat the statistic yourself; you may be challenged on it by someone who is aware that it is little more than an urban myth. It also has potentially dangerous side effects; faced with a 70 per cent chance of failure it can lead to resistance to change or even a total denial that change is the lesser of two evils. It can create a negative attitude to any (sensible) plans you create; 'you led us into a situation where we desperately need to change, you say that change is 70 per cent likely to fail, what confidence do we have that you are the person to lead us out?'

If you do need to change, simply make sure you plan for it sensibly. Chapter 38 covers a study that may help in this activity!

So what are the big takeaways here?

- Don't pass on stuff that you hear without challenging it.
- Don't blindly believe everything you see hear or read; challenge it.
- Remember that:

> 'By doubting we are led to question,
> by questioning we arrive at the truth.'
> *Peter Abelard*

Source

conversationsofchange.com.au/2013/09/02/70-of-change-projects-fail-bollocks1

See also

Chapter 1 – Spreadsheets alone do not a judgement make

Chapter 28 – What happens when you (or someone you manage) make decisions under pressure?

Chapter 38 – Learning from successful change

38 LEARNING FROM SUCCESSFUL CHANGE

Before you spend a heap of money employing a firm of 'change management consultants' read this chapter... it may save you a fortune

'Change is the only constant': we've known this since Heraclitus said it (in Greek) in around 500 BCE. Generally speaking, managing change is a bit more involved in the 21st century than it was 2,000 years ago.

IBM carried out a survey in 2013/2014 that looked at the experiences people had of deliberate change programmes, what proportion of these had been (proportionally) successful and what factors had contributed to the success.

Between September 2013 and February 2014 the researchers carried out nearly 1,400 interviews and a series of online surveys. The results represent opinions of people in 48 countries and more than 20 industries. Individuals taking part ranged from the executives who sponsored change projects through to project managers, change specialists, functional subject matter experts, other people involved specifically in the change project and people in corporate roles.

They started off (reporting the results) by sharing the figures for success of the change projects:

- 45 per cent of organizations achieved 'less than 48 per cent success' in their change projects
- 35 per cent achieved between 48 per cent and 75 per cent success in their change
- 20 per cent achieved more than 75 per cent success in their change projects.

IBM decided to call the last group, the 75 per cent+ success achievers, 'Change Architects'. They analysed what it was that these organizations did that was different to the majority and, therefore, what it was that predicted success.

They found three factors that they called: *Lead at all levels, Make change matter* and *Build the muscle*. These titles are a bit all-encompassing, so they added definition:

Lead at all levels

Success in change programmes starts from the top, but it includes the entire organization – the leadership sponsors the change, the middle management owns it and the overall culture promotes change at every level of the organization. Asked what the most important aspects of successful change were, the responses were as follows:

Top management sponsorship	83%
A shared vision	64%
Corporate culture that motivates and promotes change	57%
Honest and timely communication	53%
Ownership of change by middle management	51%
Employee involvement	46%
Change agents (pioneers of change)	39%
Efficient structure and roles within organization	27%
Skill-set of project team	24%
Efficient training programmes	18%
Adjustment of performance measures	14%
Monetary and non-monetary incentives	9%
Focus on project management tasks	7%
Regular status reports to management	6%

Note that the elements in cells that are shaded are the elements that relate to 'things', whereas the more important elements above and unshaded are about people's attitudes and behaviours.

The study then outlines the reported 'most effective means of changing attitudes and behaviours':

Involve leaders in role modelling	73%
Establish and communicate a compelling case for change	73%
Identify and empower people who are passionate about change	64%
Align performance goals	45%
Use reward and recognition systems	28%
Create top-down pressure through hierarchy	10%
Apply sanctions where necessary to achieve compliance	4%

A single statistic that is important in making these things happen is that in the Change Architects group, 64 per cent of senior managers *were held accountable* for the driving of the change agenda. In other words, it was written into their KPIs (Key Performance Indicators) and objectives, whereas in the less successful groups the figure was 45 per cent.

Another major difference between the Change Architects group and the other, less successful organizations was the relative use of employee input: 71 per cent of Change Architects seek, consider and implement employee suggestions in relation to the changes. This compares to only 52 per cent of the other organizations.

Make change matter

Critical to the success of change programmes is the clarity of vision of why the change is vital to the organization. This must be well understood throughout the whole organization and throughout the whole lifetime of the change programme.

89 per cent of respondents measured the progress of their change programme mainly against delivery milestones and through status reports of task fulfilment.

In contrast, the more successful organizations were much more likely to measure progress against such 'soft' factors as the adoption of appropriate skills and behaviours (57 per cent more often than all others), understanding of organizational benefits (52 per cent more often) of the change, commitment to personal role and case for change (50 per cent more often), and level of senior leadership support (39 per cent more often).

Build the muscle

Change is a constant but it is becoming increasingly important for organizational health.

55 per cent of the Change Architects always or regularly use a formal change management method. This compared with only 42 per cent of the less successful organizations.

36 per cent of the Change Architects trained their responsible people in the use of a formal change management method. This compares with only 28 per cent of the less successful organizations.

33 per cent of the Change Architects consolidate their change management professionals into a centre of excellence. This compares with only 24 per cent of the less successful organizations.

In other words, the organizations who treat change as a recurring constant rather than an ad hoc reaction to stimuli are more likely to manage change successfully.

The challenges associated with successfully implementing change initiatives remain heavy with 'soft factors', such as corporate culture and motivation but when asked to rate the future challenges to implementing more change, respondents saw the hard factors (marked * below) as increasingly significant.

Corporate culture	40%
*Shortage of resources (for example, budget, people)	44%
Complexity is underestimated	44%
*Change of processes	36%
*Change of IT systems	35%
Lack of commitment at higher management	23%
Lack of transparency because of wrong or missing information and communication	20%
Lack of change know-how	19%
Lack of motivation of involved employees	17%
*Technological barriers	17%

There is the data; what use can you as a leader make of it, to improve your chances of success?

First, look at your organization; has it got the 'muscle'? Are you building change management professionalism as a career path for people or is it a spare-time activity away from their day job?

Then look at your 'hard' factors. Could your ICT systems adapt to change or are they hardwired to remain rigid? How about your business processes. Could they flex or would that break the organization?

If you have change in hand at present, look back at the second table in 'Lead at all levels'. Does your senior leadership team actually role model appropriate behaviours? Are their bonuses reliant on the success of the change programme? Are the middle managers actually targeted to achieve the change or is all the onus on the 'Change Management Team'? An example the author came across in the early 2000s was an organization where the CEO had declared a need to reduce the headcount by 20 per cent through improved efficiency. After two whole years the head count actually rose by 1.5 per cent! Simply because the programme to identify and plan efficiency improvements was being handled entirely by a dedicated team and no one else was targeted to achieve a reduction in headcounts.

If you have change in hand at present and you have a dedicated team responsible for it, find out what mechanism exists for employee suggestions to support the change, if there aren't any, or they aren't working, remember that: '71 per cent of Change Architects seek, consider and implement employee suggestions in relation to the changes. This compares to only 52 per cent of the other organizations.'

You can increase the likelihood of success by widening the net to involve and include everyone.

So what are the big takeaways here?

- Spread the word that successful change is about more than successful planning; the soft factors are critical.
- Prepare yourself and your team for the management of change; work change learning and change targets into the fabric of everyone's career and day job.
- Remember that change can be successful; but not often by chance!

Source

www-935.ibm.com/services/us/gbs/bus/html/gbs-making-change-work.html

See also

Chapter 15 – Successful change begins with 'good' communication

Chapter 18 – Leadership and leaders; let's get complex

Chapter 28 – What happens when you (or someone you manage) make decisions under pressure?

Chapter 37 – 'Science, schmience'... take it with a pinch of salt

39 TRUST IN YOUR VIRTUAL TEAM

It is both important and possible to build and maintain relationships of trust between people who rarely if ever meet

It is a truth universally acknowledged that to work well with someone towards a common goal you have to have a reasonable degree of mutual trust. So what is the situation when you don't actually clap eyes on that person for a considerable percentage of the time you are supposed to be working in harmony?

Kaisa Henttonen and Kirsimarja Blomqvist, of the Lappeenranta University of Technology in Finland, set out to analyse the challenges and possibilities in building trust through technology-mediated communication in virtual teams.

Trust was defined in their study as the 'expectation of the capability, goodwill and self-reference visible in mutually beneficial behaviour enabling cooperation under risk'.

They undertook this by conducting two case studies:

Case study A was a global management team. It was a multi-state, transnational team working across multiple time zones. The 23 team members originated from Asia, USA, Australia and Europe. Eleven worked in their own home country, the remainder were either from the organization's home country working abroad or were from other nations working in the organization's home country. 58 per cent spoke English as a second language.

Case study B was a specific work team engaged in service. Its workflow was regular and ongoing. All team members were of the same nationality and spoke the same first language. The 13 permanent members were all located in the same country and time zone; in fact some were co-located in small clusters. Some had also previously worked in the same team as others. (There

were also some 'temporary' team members drafted in and out
to cope with seasonal high workloads.) All the team members
undertook similar tasks in the team and job rotation was used.

Both teams were from the same Nordic ICT company.
Approximately 40 per cent of each team took part in the study.

The participants' opinions, based on their own experiences in
global virtual teams, formed the basis for the research. This
took the form of an interview based on 21 open questions.
These questions were given to the participants in advance as
the questions were quite demanding and needed recall of past
incidents. All the interviews were carried out over less than one
month.

Case study findings

1. There usually needs to be some common trait among the
   members of a team so that they all 'fit' together. The study
   found that these common bonds can be widely varied;
   in case study A the declared rationale for the creation
   of the virtual team was to improve efficiency through a
   centralized management team rather than a disparate group
   of independent managers each managing their own site
   differently. The fact that the team members were all managers
   and all of a similar position in the hierarchy was cited as
   adequate to create that fit and confidence in each other's
   competence. In case study B, the team members were selected
   from a large pool of volunteers. The team's work was to be in
   an area thought to be full of promise and career potential. This
   shared interest and the perception that the team was a selected
   'elite' was felt to be a significant contributory factor in both
   the fit of the individual members and their immediate, innate
   perception of their teammates' capability.
2. In both cases the team members were in contact with each
   other prior to any face-to-face meeting. The language used
   in emails during this period tended to be rather formal and
   stilted with very few social cues. Once the team members
   had met, their written communications took on a more
   conversational tone. After the initial face-to-face meeting the
   volume of communication also rose. This increase in volume

and the more conversational tone were cited as contributing to increases in a feeling of trust.

3. Once the teams started functioning, the action of delivering agreed results contributed to the building of trust. This was common across both teams, even where the action of one member didn't actually impact operationally on another directly.

4. A member taking initiative and being proactive, especially in the sharing of information, contributed to the building of trust in them specifically.

5. Case study B team unanimously reported that 'social information' in addition to 'task information' helped to build trust. Theirs wasn't a universal opinion; two members of Team A were a bit sceptical that social relationships could actually form virtually, voicing the opinion that relationships need face-to-face contact in order to evolve.

6. These results concerning social communication indicate that some element of care and concern, the 'goodwill' component of trust, is present in these interactions. Also that a positive attitude towards cooperation, the 'self-reference' component of trust is also delivered via this channel.

7. Most of the Team B members suggested that a written, public record of the integrated goals and matching responsibilities helped. They also felt that all the team members should be aware of the assumptions and values behind the responsibilities.

8. Where team members were interdependent (case study B) there was evidence that when people are trusted and trusting they will make extra discretionary effort. Conversely, it was considered that if some team members refused to make discretionary effort, when in practical terms they could, it impacted directly on the trust level within the team.

9. Finally, maintaining as stable a team as possible, not constantly changing the members, was considered important.

So, there is the data; what use is it to you as a leader and manager?

Most of the nine findings listed above are also true when you are dealing with a co-located team. The obvious difference is the lack of face-to-face contact, informal visibility and the difficulties associated with information flow. Here are six logical actions that flow from the research:

- If at all possible, get a face-to-face meeting set up quickly so that the team can physically shake hands and size each other up. If this is not viable, get a good quality video-link meeting for the same purpose.
- At this initial 'kick-off', get everyone to introduce themselves and establish their individual credibility to be on the team. If you send out a heads-up about this in advance you can ask the team members to prepare a short presentation style introduction; their completion of this is a subliminal first delivery of an agreed outcome.
- Open up informal, 'social' channels of communication. Encourage people to share some personal information about themselves to make them appear more human and less distant. Don't force this and certainly avoid trying to do it before the work-related communications but actively encourage it.
- While it is clear that everyone is busy, and that your formal virtual meetings need a sensible agenda, try to get some 'less work-related' chat going. You can do this at the beginning or end of the formal progress meetings, or have separate meetings dedicated to this.
- Encourage and publicly applaud any proactive behaviour.
- Ensure that you make your communications as informal as you reasonably can; while you have to be careful to ensure that your meaning isn't lost, you can write like you speak and speak like you speak, too. Try to spread your communication media as well; communicate with team members outside the formal progress meetings on a one-to-one basis as well as addressing the group. Text a team member just to ask how things are going, or just to say thanks for a small job. Text is seen by many as an informal channel of communication.

So what are the big takeaways here?

- **Speak to your remote team members regularly;** one to one and informally, even if you've got nothing to say, ring them up and ask them how it's going.

- **Read back your emails and messages; do they sound serious and formal?** If so make a serious effort to lighten up!
- **Remember that it isn't difficult or slow to build trust in a virtual team;** it just takes a bit more intelligent and concerted activity.

Source

www2.warwick.ac.uk/fac/soc/wbs/conf/olkc/archive/oklc5/papers/e-3_henttonen.pdf

See also

Chapter 1 – Spreadsheets alone do not a judgement make

Chapter 3 – It ain't what you say, it's the way that you say it

Chapter 11 – To follow me they have to be able to see me, right?

Chapter 12 – It takes all sorts to make a world

Chapter 21 – Management and leadership... a hot topic! But for whom?

Chapter 23 – We're working nine to five – it's no way to make a living

Chapter 32 – ROWE, ROWE, ROWE your boat!

40 YOU CAN *NOT* BE SERIOUS!

'Some people think work is a matter of life or death, this is disappointing; I can assure you it is far more serious than that.'

With apologies to Bill Shankly

With all the responsibility that goes with it, being a leader is no laughing matter. Running a business is a serious business, and frivolity should be kept away from the day-to-day challenges of striving for success.

Or should it?

Humour is common to almost all human interaction and consequently has an impact on work teams and larger organizations. Sadly, most managers and leaders fail to take the subject of humour seriously. Often they simply reject its numerous benefits. Humour is a multifunctional management tool that can be used to achieve many objectives.

Eric Romero of Intrepid Consulting and Kevin Cruthirds, lecturer in the Department of Management at the University of Texas, published an enlightening (and enlightened) document in 2006. It was wittily entitled: 'The Use of Humor in the Workplace.'

The article is a careful study of a range of other academic works, rather than a single piece of original research in its own right. As such, it draws on numerous credible sources and it presents a selection of findings that demonstrate the value of humour to managers and leaders, even in the dark times of recession and economic gloom and doom.

Without peppering this chapter with the original references, here are ten ways that humour can benefit a leader or an organization:

1. Senior team members (not just managers but members with more seniority; i.e. the ones who have been on the team longest) often feel an understandable and laudable desire to maintain the team's identity and integrity. They often use mildly aggressive humour; good-natured teasing, light ridicule, a bit of mockery, on the greenhorns. This helps to shape their behaviours to conform to the team's norms. It also ensures that they prove themselves worthy of their membership of the team. Once the newbies conform, they are accepted as full members of the team and the ribbing fades away. Having undergone the initiation they are now proud of their acceptance and defensive of the team.

2. Group cohesiveness can be achieved and improved both through positive reinforcement within the group and the reduction of any external threat. For example, in a group faced with the threat of external competition, people often use aggressive humour by making jokes about their competitors. By deriding the competition, the group members are placing themselves above the threat and, in doing so, perceive a feeling of triumph over it.

3. Shared laughter and a bit of fun helps the bonding process. This enables team members to stick together in the face of adversity. People need to support and rely on each other to complete projects or hit targets.

4. Humour also has a positive effect by making interactions less tense. This aids communication by creating a more open atmosphere which enhances listening, increases the likely acceptance of the message and improves understanding. Humour has an 'attention-getting' quality that aids comprehension and assists in persuasion.

5. Moderate, self-deprecating humour can help a person of high organizational status to identify (and be identified) with their 'audience'. This helps to lower hierarchical barriers by reducing tension and temporarily reducing the speaker's status.

6. Humour can also be used to enhance a person's power in a hierarchical relationship. The freedom to use humour is often associated with higher status people; so the person making the witty comments must be the boss!

7. Humour can allow one to critique without producing

negative interpersonal effects. It can reduce the resistance people usually feel when they are critiqued because they can laugh with the person offering the light-hearted criticism. Shared humour is inconsistent with taking offence, so it often aids freer and more honest communication.

8. There is strong evidence that humour reduces stress. Joking about a stressful situation distracts people from fear and develops a sense of control over it. This can be both for the person who makes the humorous comment and the others 'in the same boat' who hear the comment and find it gives them both a sense of control and a feeling that they are not facing it alone.

9. Humour is linked to improved creative thinking; it promotes openness to new ideas by relaxing people and making them less likely to criticize mistakes or reject new ideas. #6 above leads to a safer environment for people to act on new ideas more freely. Individuals in a humorous environment are more likely to engage in creative problem-solving as well as direct creativity.

10. Humour can be successfully used to make dull but important routine tasks more interesting.

The study defined different types of humour: self-deprecating humour, aggressive humour (both full-blooded aggressive and mild-aggressive), affiliative humour and self-enhancing humour. Obviously, the different types have different effects in different situations and therefore the wrong type of humour in the wrong place can be destructive.

Humour can also be used to encourage people to use/access/ want to attend learning and support material. In a 2005 article published in *Teaching of Psychology*, professors Mark Shatz and Frank LoSchiavo reported that when the designers inserted a range of humorous and light-hearted elements into an online course, students logged on more often because they were more likely to enjoy the experience.

OK, there is the research, what use is it to you as a leader?

Think about the situations that you face every day: managing people's performance, defining strategies, setting objectives, handling downsizing or budget cuts, selling to customers, dealing with people conflicts, solving problems or building your team. Where might you be able to engender a bit more cohesiveness, or generate a bit more creativity by injecting just a smidgen of humour? How might you be able to calm down an irate client, or improve someone's performance by using a light-hearted analogy?

If you have to put together a presentation to the board, or to the staff, or to fellow managers, could you find some suitably humorous images to slip into the slides to help people to accept and remember your content (who knows, you might be able to keep them awake through the presentation as well!)

> *'People learn nothing when they're asleep and very little when they're bored.'*
> *John Cleese*

Mr Cleese put his money where his mouth is and in 1972 was a founder member of the company Video Arts. It is still going strong more than 40 years later. Watch some of their training videos; they prove that business and management are too serious a pair of subjects to be all dull and worthy about.

So what are the big takeaways here?

- **Encourage other people to lighten up as well.** 'Gravitas' may be seen as important in leadership, but a bit of levity can induce any of the ten benefits listed earlier.
- **Keep a sense of humour about you and use it;** you don't have to become a stand-up comedian in order to reap some of these benefits. Just try not to take every situation you encounter as if you were an undertaker with toothache.
- **Remember that this chapter is based on research done by academics;** people who have chosen to work most of their lives with people who haven't yet grown up.

Sources

rspb.royalsocietypublishing.org/content/early/2011/09/19/
rspb.2011.1373

www.apa.org/monitor/jun06/learning.aspx

stress.about.com/od/stresshealth/a/laughter.htm

ww2.valdosta.edu/~mschnake/RomeroCruthirds2006.pdf

See also

Chapter 1 – Spreadsheets alone do not a judgement make

Chapter 3 – It ain't what you say, it's the way that you say it

Chapter 5 – 'Workers' play time' – is it really worth it?

Chapter 12 – It takes all sorts to make a world

Chapter 33 – Find out what your followers think about you, and talk to them about it!

INDEX

feedback, 35, 119, 150–1, 157–8, 180, 189–93
Flesch-Kincaid Grade Level, 23, 25
Flesch Reading Ease test, 23–4
Flesh, Rudolf, 22–3, 24
full-time workers, 130–1, 133

Generation Y workers, 148–52, *see also* millennial generation
Goodman, John, 107–11
grammar check, 24–5
green working environment, 97–101
group cohesiveness, 228, 230
groupthink, 142–6

happy employees and productivity, 27–31, 64
home workers, 62–6
house plants, 97–101
HR, 11, 12, 36–7, 76, 77, 112, 123–4, 126–7
humour, 227–30

IBM, 216–18
identifying with employer, 41, 42, 52, 54, 64
'implementer' team role, 69
influence, 2–5, 39, 76, 134, 139, 214
informal learning, 151, 155–60
Institute of Business Ethics, 200–1

Janis, Irving, 142–3
job satisfaction, 39, 40, 41, 42, 64, 117, 139–40

knowledge economy, 102, 105

leader-learner, 36–7
leaders, 102, 105–6
   developing, 33–8
leadership, 102–6, 121–2
   adaptive leadership, 103–4
   administrative leadership, 104
   enabling leadership, 104–5
leader-teacher, 36–8
'lean' working environment, 97–100
learning, 82
   action, 36, 37
   informal, 151, 155–60
   on the job, 153–60
   sources, 153–4
life goals, 56, 60

listening, 19, 120–2, 134, 136–40, 189, 192
logos, 3, 4–5, 39, 214
long-term absences, 76
luck, 45–9
luck school, 49
lucky hunches, 47–8

management skills, 118–22, 137, 191–3
   talent management, 195–9
managers, 117–22
managers' perceptions of staff, 9
Mattel, 202
MBTI, *see* Myers-Briggs Type Indicator
meetings, 178–82
memory, 82
mentoring, 151, 158
micro-businesses, 176
millennial generation, 173
   and attitudes to work, 174–5
   see also Generation Y workers
mis-selling, 108
Model of Proof, 2–3, 4, 213–14
'monitor/evaluator' team role, 69
motivation, 7–12, 17
Myers-Briggs Type Indicator, 112–16

National Institute of Adult Continuing Education, *see* NIACE
neuroscience, 80–1, 82
NIACE, 24, 25, 26
night workers, 131–2
office air quality, *see* air quality

office environment, 39–43, 97–101, *see also* green working environment; workspaces
on-the-job training, 153–4, 159
owner/managers, 130–1

part-time workers, 130–1, 133
pathos, 4–5, 39, 214
peer-to-peer communication, 158
people management skills, 118, 121–2
'plant' team role, 68
Plato's Academy, 1
PowerPoint®, 5, 206–11
praise, 121
presenteeism, 74, 75
private sector absenteeism, 74
productive meetings, 180–2

GENIUS

Bring a little genius into your day.

SO MUCH OF WHAT YOU'VE BEEN TOLD ABOUT BUSINESS IS WRONG . . .

Too many theories, not enough real-world evidence. The *Genius* series cuts through the noise to bring you proven research from around the world that you can use to reach your goals at work.

INNOVATIVE: *Genius* is the only series of business books that is based on actual research, rather than the opinions and preconceptions of the author.

IN-DEPTH: Our authors have read thousands of journal articles, books and pieces of research, so that you don't have to. The 40 most compelling insights each form a chapter of their *Genius* title.

PRACTICAL: As well as explaining the research, the *Genius* series shows you practical ways to implement these in a business setting.

UNRIVALLED: Our authors are leading authorities in their respective fields — their teachings will improve your work and business skills.

COMING SUMMER 2015

ISBN: 9781473615007
RRP: £12.99, Paperback

ISBN: 9781473605367
RRP: £12.99, Paperback

ISBN: 9781473605381
RRP: £12.99, Paperback

ABOUT THE BOOKS

Presentation, sales and strategy are topics surrounded by myths and received wisdom, but it doesn't have to be that way. The *Genius* series brings together 40 proven pieces of research in one place and shows how to implement them to achieve success.

ABOUT THE AUTHORS

Simon Raybould is a speaker and trainer. As a speaker, he specialises in resilience, emotional robustness, public speaking and presenting. As a trainer, he is the director of the training company Aware Plus. He worked for 24 years as a university researcher, publishing in many peer-reviewed journals and developing an international reputation.

Graham Jones is a leading authority on the science of selling. He is a Member of the British Psychological Society, a Visiting Lecturer at University of Buckingham Business School, and an Associate Lecturer at the Open University. He has written more than 20 books, which have been translated around the world.

Richard Jones is a strategic and change management consultant and entrepreneur in the field of telecoms and technology. He has consulted at board and government level on projects from Kazakhstan to Kansas and from Curacao to Colombo. He has co-founded several different companies, one of which was acquired for 45 million GBP, another of which floated on the Nasdaq, and another has now received 50 million USD of investment.

JOHN
MURRAY
LEARNING

@_JMLearning